P9-CQN-390

"I'm so excited about this book, *Loving Life as an At-Home Mom*. Donna has put LOVE and lots of HEART into her message to women. Her home and life have been BEAUTIFUL, GODLY EXAMPLES of what an at-home mom can do and become. I feel fully this is a book women need to read."

Emilie Barnes, Founder and author
of *More Hours in My Day*

"At a time when at-home mothers are valued about the same as a bad episode from a 'Donna Reed' rerun, this book offers them the STATUS and ESTEEM they deserve. Donna Otto recognizes the WORK OF A MOTHER for what it truly is—the MOST SACRED TRUST THAT GOD could ever give to a woman."

Dr. Tim Kimmel, Family Matters Ministry

"I never read any of Donna's works without vowing to be MORE EFFICIENT, more time-management effective, more prioritized. This book is a WONDERFUL TOOL for moms who stay at home or for those of us who wish we could stay at home!"

Karen B. Mains, author,
Open Heart, Open Home

"For seven years we have watched Donna Otto's STRONG COMMITMENT TO CHRIST and to her family. She's a person who's committed to honoring others and we HIGHLY RECOMMEND HER MINISTRY AND MESSAGE in *Loving Life as an At-Home Mom*."

Gary Smalley & **John Trent,** authors,
The Blessing and *Home Remedies*

loving
life *as an*
at-home
mom

[handwritten inscription: 2009 Dear Michelle, Love your Mothering Aunt Otto]

Donna Otto

HARVEST HOUSE PUBLISHERS

EUGENE, OREGON

Unless otherwise indicated, Scripture quotes are taken from the New American Standard Bible, © 1960, 1962, 1963, 1968, 1971, 1972, 1973, 1975, 1977 by The Lockman Foundation. Used by permission.

Scripture quotations marked NKJV are taken from the New King James Version, Copyright © 1979, 1980, 1982 by Thomas Nelson, Inc. Used by permission. All rights reserved.

Scripture quotations marked ESV are taken from The Holy Bible, English Standard Version, copyright © 2001 by Crossway Bibles, a division of Good News Publishers. Used by permission. All rights reserved.

Every effort has been made to give proper credit for all stories, poems, and quotations. If for any reason proper credit has not been given, please notify the author or publisher and proper notation will be given on future printing.

Cover by Terry Dugan Design, Bloomington, Minnesota

Cover photo © IT Stock Free/Jupiterimages

LOVING LIFE AS AN AT-HOME MOM
Portions of this book were excerpted from *The Stay-at-Home-Mom*
Copyright © 2006 by Donna Otto
Published by Harvest House Publishers
Eugene, Oregon 97402
www.harvesthousepublishers.com

Library of Congress Cataloging-in-Publication Data
Otto, Donna.
   Loving life as an at-home mom / Donna Otto. -- Rev. and expanded.
      p. cm.
   Rev. ed. of: The stay at home mom. Rev. & expanded. Eugene, Or. : Harvest House Publishers, c1997.

   ISBN-13: 978-0-7369-1817-6 (pbk.)
   ISBN-10: 0-7369-1817-5

   1. Mothers--United States. 2. Housewives--United States. 3. Motherhood--United States. 4. Motherhood--Religious aspects--Christianity. I. Otto, Donna. Stay at home mom. II. Title.
HQ759O887 2006
306.874'3--dc22

                                    2006021453

All rights reserved. No part of this publication may be reproduced, stored in a retrieval system, or transmitted in any form or by any means—electronic, mechanical, digital, photocopy, recording, or any other—except for brief quotations in printed reviews, without the prior permission of the publisher.

Printed in the United States of America

06 07 08 09 10 11 12 / LB-SK / 10 9 8 7 6 5 4 3 2 1

OVERTON MEMORIAL LIBRARY
HERITAGE CHRISTIAN UNIVERSITY
P.O. Box HCU
Florence, Alabama 35630

To the women of
Homemakers By Choice
who support at-home moms everywhere.

Thank you, Harvest House staff. Every department is needed to move a book from the author's desk to the readers' hands and hearts.

Bob Hawkins, president of Harvest House, your unending support for this message to stay-at-home moms is noted and needed. Thank you for the gift of that support to me personally. May this book be a blessing to you.

Thank you to Lars and Elisabeth Elliot Gren. Elisabeth, thank you for writing the message of the Foreword on my heart.

Anissa Hamlin, my research assistant.

Amy Malouf, friend and contributor.

Barb Gordon, you made it happen. Thank you.

contents

foreword

Women who are willing to stay at home to do "nothing more than" mother their children need all the help they can get. I am glad Donna Otto is solidly on their side and has written a book that will certainly help them.

The movement that was meant to liberate women has not been a thundering success. Women are coming to see that the elusive fulfillment everyone seeks is not to be found in the office any more than it is to be found in the kitchen (and of course men could have told us that if we had listened!). Fulfillment in its truest sense is to be found in surrender and obedience. We need only look at two models for the proof: Eve, whose motto was "My will be done," who thus brought sorrow and death to the world, and Mary, who said, "Thy will be done," and by being willing simply to be somebody's mother, cooperated with God in bringing salvation to the world. No woman has ever been so highly exalted.

Donna Otto is one of those older women who, according to the Bible, are meant to encourage and set an example for younger women, helping them not only to love their husbands and children, but also to stay home.

For a woman to stay home in America today takes the courage to face rude questions, criticism, even ostracism at times. It usually takes a willingness on the part of both her and her husband to make material sacrifices. The conviction that this is the course God wants her to follow will give the needed courage.

It is my prayer that many readers will be strengthened and encouraged in their convictions, and that many more will gain a new perspective hitherto undreamed of, not merely of the importance but of the glory of full-time mothering.

Elisabeth Elliot,
author of 40 books,
Magnolia, MA

introduction

There is a change in America—again! The change is reminiscent of the 1950s, with mashed potatoes and meatloaf making a comeback. But the change is more intentional, lead by the generation of men and women born in the 70s. House and garden and home makeover shows abound on TV, Internet blogs are popping up with how-to helps ranging from how many towels we should own to what is the best floor cleaner to use. These blogs receive thousands of hits daily. Food channels are in abundance 24 hours a day. Rachel Ray, a 37-year-old chef and cookbook author, has garnered an unprecedented mass appeal in America. Martha Stewart, now out of prison, is back on the magazine racks and TV screens espousing home and domestic life. High-end stores like Williams Sonoma are offering a rotary iron (known as a mangle in my day) for tablecloths, sheets, and flat linens. (Only ten years ago many young families didn't even own an iron.) Middle-income stores offer the widest offering of kitchen gadgets in 30 years. Oprah espouses the advantages of home and family life daily.

It has been more than 20 years since I determined to spend some of my life helping young women navigate the early stages of...

- womanhood
- motherhood
- marriage
- creating a home

My passion continues to grow.

I offer this book to give you courage to make the choices necessary to be an at-home mom. Additionally, you'll find practical encouragements for daily life. Once upon a time, the at-home mom made a home that fed, washed, and slept her family. In the twenty-first century, an at-home mom teaches, works, handles all the technology, shreds paper for protection from identity theft, and watches over her children because of prevalent "stranger danger" situations. And so much more!

Sometimes this job called "at-home mom" requires giving up. Giving up a dream, a career, relationships, education, and freedom. Few people can successfully hold down two full-time positions at one time. I want to assure you that the choice to invest in your marriage, children, and home will reap great rewards. This fact was addressed by a woman who heard me speak more than 15 years ago and sent the following note:

> I wish I was better with words, but I just wanted to say thank you today as I am about to celebrate my 15th wedding anniversary. I don't think I would be here today if I hadn't made the choice of letting go of a dream and being the wife God wanted me to be— not that it has been easy...But thank you! Your words were strong and clear. I love my husband and family and see the years I have just spent as an amazing investment. Letting go was hard, but the results have been rich.

So whether you are letting go, giving up, or starting out, the truth is you are building up for the future by making the choice to be an at-home mom today.

Looking up,
Donna Otto

1

loving life

For a woman at home with children, life isn't always lovely. You know that, and I do too. I had the challenge of raising a strong-willed daughter who now is a mom herself. As a speaker to women's groups around the country, I also hear weekly from young mothers about the joys, challenges, and heartbreaks of being at home with children.

Mindy is a mom I particularly remember. She came to me with tears in her big brown eyes and a look that would melt the coldest heart. She was desperate for encouragement and hope. She was an educated woman who had left a stimulating and exciting job to make her full-time job motherhood. Her world, once large and exciting, suddenly seemed very small: small house, small children, small budget, small wardrobe, and incessant small talk, usually at the three-year-old level. "Help!" Mindy cried. "Surely life is more than this! How can I survive?" Mindy's story is repeated wherever I go. The situation differs, of course, but the theme is the same: "Help!"

Is this you? I call this book *loving life as an at-home mom* because, as an older woman who mentors young moms, I know some secrets. One has to do with the choices we make. One choice is choosing to love the life you have, especially as a mom at home, even when circumstances seem to squeeze some of the joy out of your day. Loving life is not just a dream; it's possible and real. This book is for you from one who has traveled your road and counseled many young moms who are right where you are now.

Loving life as a mom at home involves understanding and embracing the four major facets of most full-time, at-home moms:

- You are a unique woman.
- You are a wife.
- You are a mom.
- You maintain a home.

We will look at each of these facets in the following pages. I've included lots of tips and suggestions for you to consider and follow. You'll discover some pitfalls to avoid. Success stories from women like you will encourage you. Best of all, you will know that you are not alone—and the sweet gift you have as a mom at home can create a legacy that will resonate from generation to generation. This season of your life as a mother at home can be the richest and best you'll ever enjoy. That's why loving life as a woman, wife, homemaker, and mother at home is possible and within reach.

But first, let's step back and look at your decision to be at home. There is a lot involved. Some of it has deep meaning beyond even the practical steps you considered when deciding with your husband to stay at home.

2

you are not alone

One Saturday morning when her husband, Mark, was out of town, Kim e-mailed her neighbor Mary and asked to meet at a local coffee shop. The two women had become friends even though Mary, the mother of three grown sons, was nearly 30 years older than Kim. Mary saw in Kim the daughter she never had; and Kim was attracted to Mary's motherly warmth and wisdom.

Kim's voice sounded a little quavery to Mary over the phone, so she hurried to Starbucks.

"I'm pregnant," Kim blurted tearfully when Mary arrived.

Mary hugged her tenderly for a moment and then said, "That's wonderful news! But be honest with me, Kim. Are these tears of joy or disappointment?"

"A little bit of both, I guess," Kim answered, wiping her eyes with a tissue. "Mark and I want a family, but we were hoping to wait a few years. We have some financial goals to achieve and careers to establish. My parents paid a bundle for my education, and they're expecting me to be the district attorney some day. Mark and I are thrilled about the prospect of being parents, but this baby is really throwing us a curve by showing up early."

After their first cup of coffee and a discussion of baby names, Kim sighed deeply. "I need to ask you a question that Mark and I haven't talked about yet. It's something that's been on my mind since the moment the pregnancy test came back positive. I'm wondering if I should stay at home to raise my child. Did you work when your kids were small?"

"When my boys were growing up, moms staying at home to raise their children was more common than today. Yet like you and Mark, Sam and I had financial and career goals. So a month after our Robby was born, I dropped him off at my mother's and returned to my job as a medical technician. When Ricky was born two years later, I was off work for six weeks, and then I was dropping two kids off at Grandma's or the babysitter's.

"Then I began to realize that Robby and Ricky were spending more time with other people than they were with me, the person who was responsible for raising them. That really bothered me. It wasn't right. So when I became pregnant with Tommy a few months later, I decided to quit my job when he was born and be a full-time mom."

"What did Sam say about that?" Kim asked. "I'm not sure Mark will want to postpone some of our financial goals so I can stay at home."

"Sam and I talked about it for several weeks while I was carrying Tommy. I assured him that I would do what I could to help us stay on target for early retirement. And after I quit my job it took us both awhile to adjust to some of the money-saving measures we had to adopt. But we made it. I went back to work part-time when Tommy entered high school, and here we are getting ready to retire and travel."

"Didn't you miss the stimulation of a career and the friends you had at work?" Kim pressed, mirroring her own concerns.

"Of course I did. I had a good job with a future in healthcare. I'm not saying it was an easy choice. There were sacrifices. But I knew it was the right thing to do for our boys. It was God's best design for raising them."

"I don't know, Mary," Kim said. "Staying at home with my kids would be wonderful, but there's so much at stake."

"What's at stake are your kids, Kim. Think about what your life is going to look like in 15 or 20 years. What do you want for your children? Read the data and check the facts. Children raised by an intentional at-home mom are going to be more responsive and cooperative than children shuffled between home and daycare.

"You may sacrifice something, such as your career, but you have the opportunity to make the courageous choice that I wish I had made with my first child instead of my third. You can't go back in time and make this choice later, Kim. If I were in your shoes, I would jump at the chance to be an at-home mom."

staying at home: an idea whose time has come

Perhaps you picked up this book because you're going through, or have just gone through, an experience like Kim's. You're the mother of a young child or you're soon going to be a mom. You may have an expensive education behind you and a promising career before you that you don't want to waste. Or maybe you and your husband have a budget that could become a monster if you stopped working.

Yet you look at your young child (or pat the child-to-be in your tummy) and wonder who's going to raise him or her if you don't stay home. Grandmas and aunties are wonderful, but you know they can't care for your child like you can. Babysitters and childcare centers are convenient, but they can't come close to nurturing and training your child like you can. You see lots of moms carrying on with their careers while someone else raises their kids, but you know that God designed you to be the primary caregiver in your child's life. Should you be an at-home mom or not?

Allow me to be a Mary in your life. If I could, I would hold your hand, pat your face, hug your neck, and tell you what I tell almost every mother of young children I meet, whether at the market, on the street, in the airport, or in one of my conferences. I would tell you to join the growing ranks of moms who are making the courageous choice to stay at home and invest themselves in their kids. I would encourage you to find out how staying at home works for you. God wants you to trust Him to help you do it.

Just how large is this growing number of stay-at-home moms in the land? Here are a few facts gathered from a number of resources that should further encourage you that you are not alone in your desire to be an at-home mom.

An October 2004 *Parents* magazine article entitled "Why I Quit My Job" asserted that 87 percent of U.S. mothers with children under 12 who work outside the home would choose to stay home if they could afford to. The U.S. Census Bureau reports for 2002 that about 60 percent of all households with children under six years of age had both parents in the labor force. That number dropped to 59 percent in 2003. According to the Census Bureau, the number of stay-at-home moms grew in 2003 to an estimated 5.4 million. This was the first ever analysis of stay-at-home parents by the government agency. They also report that there were 23 million married couple households in the U.S., so approximately 23 percent of American households had a stay-at-home mom.

In a 2000 survey of 2,000 Americans, more than 60 percent of the women questioned said they would rather stay at home with their children if their finances allowed.

Many women who take maternity leave from their jobs are deciding to stay home permanently. They say family demands will keep them from returning. Some women say their decision to leave business is less a rejection of the corporate world than a realization that they have only one chance to bring up their children—and many said they feel more comfortable exercising an option that a decade ago might have been unfashionable.

the case of the missing 20- to 24-year-old woman

The Bureau of Labor Statistics figures show that there is an employment drop-off among women, particularly ages 20 to 24. The numbers have risen and then dropped significantly.

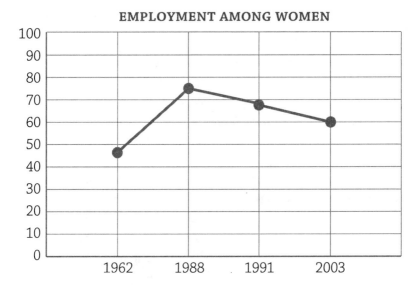

EMPLOYMENT AMONG WOMEN

Much of the reason for this decline is related to high daycare costs (much of that by government regulations in daycare) and low interest rates.

The U.S. Census Bureau released the American Family and Living Arrangement report, dated November 30, 2004, that showed stay-at-home parents topped 5.5 million: 5.4 million moms and 98,000 dads.

stories, i hear stories

Wherever I go I hear stories that reveal the hearts of women, including their struggles and their joys. These stories have affected my life, and I think they will affect and encourage you also. Let me share some of these insights from Christian women who are striving to follow what they believe is God's voice regarding raising their children, making their homes, and loving their husbands by being—or working toward being—full-time moms. In my travels I have the joy and privilege of talking and listening to thousands of moms just like you. Hear the chorus of encouragement for at-home moms from women and men who have been there. If you desire to stay at home, you are not alone.

Here are just a few of the women I've met who have adjusted or given up their careers to be stay-at-home moms:

• Karen from Connecticut has been a widowed mother for more than four years: "I'm working out of my home and homeschooling my children. It's crazy, but God makes it possible. He's our provider. It's a sacrifice, but it's the best one I've ever made. I'm an architect, and God is helping me grow professionally working at home. But I also bake cookies, and I will do anything else for my kids."

• Dina from New Jersey gave up a six-figure income when she sold her executive search firm to work part-time and have kids. She is now at home full time with her young son and daughter.

• At age 32, Sally from Phoenix gave up a high-paying job to have her first baby and stay at home with him. The pressure she experienced from her former coworkers was tremendous. Every day for 30 days straight they hounded her. Her coworkers couldn't believe she would give up such a lucrative career, insisting that she could work and be a mother. Her boss said, "I'll give you anything you want if you'll just come back to work." Her former employer's competitors offered her all she had before and more to work for them. But Sally held on to God's vision for her, and she's glad she did.

• Nicole from California gave birth to a daughter. As assistant buyer for a large department store chain, she wanted to hold on to her career. But childcare costs cut her salary in half. She decided that her job was too stressful for the reduced income and the time she was away from her daughter. She's now an at-home mom and has decided not to return to work.

• Jane Pauley, former coanchor of NBC's *Today Show,* won the applause of millions for artfully balancing family and career. Pauley stepped away from one of the highest profile jobs in television so she could be home with her young children. Now that her children are older, she has her own talk show.

• Debra from the Bronx, New York, has a teen-aged girl and two younger boys. She says, "I have never worked, and I have had such wonderful experiences with my children."

• Jean, a 75-year-old mother from Phoenix, gets right to the point: "I don't like the fact that women work today. I think a mother belongs at home. When my son would come home from school, the first word out of his mouth was 'Mom.' He expected me to be there, and I was."

A 2005 *New York Times* article captured the trend toward valuing motherhood with an article titled "Many Women at Elite Colleges Set Career Path to Motherhood."[1]

What about couples who couldn't afford an at-home mom? Here are some responses from at-home moms.

• Angela, a stay-at-home mom in New York, wonders if work makes sense at all for a mother today, considering taxes on joint income, wardrobe expenses for the working mom, and childcare costs. "You don't need a pencil and paper to figure that you're not taking home very much money after expenses. Add to that the disadvantages of being away from home many hours a day and being knocked out when you are home. It really wasn't worth it to me. I tried it, but now I'm at home."

• Deborah Fallows was a part-time professional with a Ph.D. in linguistics who gave up her career to stay home with her children. In her spare time she wrote a book, *A Mother's Work*. She states, "Although economics certainly plays an important role in a woman's decision to work, money is by no means the only or always the most important factor. Many families decide that the cost of one income, which is mainly financial, is easier to bear than the emotional costs of trying to earn two."[2]

• Virginia from Jersey City, the mother of an infant daughter, had to work through the pressure of giving up her income to stay at home. "The whole time I was pregnant I had the desire to stay home and raise my baby. But when she finally arrived I had a desire to go back into the business world. So many of our friends have their own homes and two cars. I sometimes feel that the only way my husband and I can achieve these things is for me to go back to work. Thanks for encouraging me to focus on the benefits of staying at home with my daughter."

• Terri and her husband believed it was God's will for her to stay home with their young children. Kevin's meager salary as an accountant kept them at a survival level, and he couldn't land a higher-paying management position because he didn't have a college degree. But Terri stayed home, trusting God to meet their needs.

One day Kevin received a job offer to manage an accounting office in a small community in the same state. His salary jumped and their cost of living dropped. Terri says, "I just know Kevin's new job was an answer from God as we obeyed what we believed was His plan for us."

• Chris, a gentleman from New York, reports, "My wife and I wondered before we had children if we would have sufficient income to allow her to stay at home. But we decided it was God's will that we have kids and raise them according to His Word and His ways. And we believed we would know what was best for them because God was entrusting them to us. So she stayed home.

"After six years we have proven that God will provide despite the economic circumstances. It all comes back to making sure you are in the center of God's will. We have two boys. One just started school, so my wife has taken a part-time job. With one son still at home, we have arranged our schedules so that one of us is at home with him while the other is at work. There's nothing more important to us as parents than giving our boys the security that Mom and Dad will always be here for them."

• Susie, an at-home mom from Chicago, says: "Before we had children, it didn't seem to us that we could afford for me to stay home. And at first it really wasn't even my desire to stay at home. But as soon as I had my first baby, God put it on my heart to stay at home. Somehow He managed to allow us to do it. It wasn't easy. When you try to figure out how to make things work, it's hard to let go and let God be your sustainer and help you find ways to do it. When we didn't have any money, people showed up and gave us what we needed. Things just kept coming in. So we let go even more and turned our needs over to the Lord. He always made a way for us and allowed me to stay at home."

• Joe, a husband from Portland, Oregon, comments, "We have always tried to raise our children in the right way so when they get older they are able to take the right steps. We thank God that when we first had our children—we have two, a girl and a boy—my wife was able to spend time with them at home the first few years. In the beginning I couldn't understand how we could do it, considering the financial circumstances we were under. But I let my wife do what she thought was best. It worked out, and I think we should spend more time at home with our kids."

• Sonia from New Jersey has four children. She has two perspectives of being an at-home mom: "When my first child was two months old I went back to work until he was 13. That's when I became pregnant with my second child, a daughter. Now my son is 26 and my daughter is 13, and we have two more kids, aged 10 and 8. Having been a working mom and a stay-at-home mom, I feel it's an advantage being at home. I missed being home when my first child was growing up, but it's been a blessing being here during his teenage and college years. And it's wonderful being home as the other three grow up. It's been a financial struggle at times, but the Scriptures say our God shall supply all our needs according to His riches in glory in Christ Jesus."

• Ruth from Boise, Idaho, says: "I had my first baby a few months ago, and I really had a hard time deciding whether I was going to stay home. For one thing, I actually earned a bigger salary than my husband. The financial commitment was a big part of our decision. But as I watch our little Brittany grow up each day, I'm so glad I'm here to see all the new things she's learning. I wouldn't give that up for anything."

the image of the at-home mom

Some mothers were concerned about the *image* of the at-home mom...

• Val from San Diego admits, "As a mother at home, I'm generally ignored and not thought very highly of by others. I've been told there are better things I could be doing with my time than caring for my children. But there aren't. It's a long-term investment to stay home with my youngsters, but I can see the rewards after only three years."

• Vicki, a stay-at-home mom from Amarillo, Texas, says she used to feel ignored and isolated. But it doesn't bother her anymore: "I really want to be at home. My background is in education, so I'm having a lot of fun being with my children. I understand how at-home moms can feel ignored and isolated. But the rewards far outweigh the liabilities."

• Cookie, a mother from Brooklyn, admits, "I made the decision to be a stay-at-home mom a long time ago. My son is 16 years old now, and I wasn't popular at all for staying home to raise him. I wasn't even respected by my own friends. But when my son came home from school every day, I was there.

"I just want to encourage mothers who are trying to make that decision to go to the Word of God. It will give you the answer. What we receive from our children, even by sacrificing our jobs and the esteem of our friends, is so much more than we can receive by striving to become successful, respected women."

• In her address to the students at Wellesley College, former First Lady Barbara Bush, who is also the mother of an American president, emphasized:

> As important as your obligations as a doctor, lawyer, or business leader will be, you are a human being first and those human connections with spouses, with children, with friends are the most important investments you will ever make.
>
> At the end of your life, you will never regret not having passed one more test, not winning one more verdict, or not closing one more deal. You will regret time not spent with a husband, a friend, a child, or a parent...If you have children, they must come first. Your success as a family, our success as a society, depends not on what happens at the White House, but on what happens inside your house.[3]

• Susan from Arizona isn't worried about her image as an at-home mom: "I find my home job with my daughter, Bethany, very fulfilling. I'll never forget the first time I nursed Bethany. She taught me what to do, while I was wondering if I could. I love the way she touches my side, tickling me with her little fingers. She's always happy when I feed her. When I say her name, she turns her head and looks at me. To me there's a kind of humbling awe in that. My mom was at home full time, and she was never a mindless little housewife. I won't be either."[4]

Echoing this sentiment, Elizabeth Berg says, "When asked, 'What do you do?' I still prefer proudly declaring, 'I am a stay-at-home mother,' followed by, 'Brain surgery, that's what I do—noninvasive brain surgery. Instilling important images and creating lifelong values.'"

I could tell you story after story like these. You are hearing the voices of mothers and fathers who have asked the same questions you have asked, made the same choice you have made or want to make, and certainly have made the same personal sacrifices you are making or will make to stay home with your kids. I hope you feel comforted and supported knowing you are not alone in your desire to be an at-home mom.

As you read through this book, we will discuss some of the concerns you may have about being a full-time mom: financial worries, negative images of a stay-at-home mom, lack of support from your husband or family or friends, fear of boredom and/or isolation, and simply managing the day-to-day details of home and family life.

3

you are the best choice

Abraham Lincoln's mother, Nancy Lincoln,
died when Abraham was 10.
But Lincoln, until his own death, spoke
reverently about his mother and credited
her with his intellectual stimulation. She
walked miles herself to get Abe books.

The word "choice" is what I call a perspective word. The "right to choose" and "making the right choice" are phrases fraught with subtle double meanings. The feminist movement has chosen to pit a woman who chooses to stay at home full-time against the woman who chooses to work. This phenomenon is often called the "mommy wars."[1] Choice is just that—the ability to make your own decision. I am firmly in favor of women (parents) making the choice to have children, but if you choose to have children then you also are choosing to be responsible for their care and training.

In this "for" and "against" position, women are feeling the pressure to take up sides. While all the choice issues fly, we are forgetting that every marriage and parenting situation is not alike. I had (and still do) boundless energy (God-given and in young life driven by an abundance of caffeine). My husband, David, and I also had one child who was healthy and fairly independant. I have always loved to "work." These factors allowed me to choose involvement outside of the home to a greater degree than my friend with low energy and six children. Additionally, my marriage style, based on David's and my personalities, always had elements of "independent work-style."

accommodations

Dr. Laura Schlessinger, who refers to herself as "I am my kid's mom," describes how she adjusted her work habits to accommodate availability to her motherhood desires. In the twenty-first century, with all the available technology and globalization, you can live in India and work for a company in Kansas. Certainly a mother who desires to put the raising of her children as her first choice can live *and* work in Kansas, while she chooses to raise her children.

Make your choice carefully with good counsel and accurate information. Raising a child is a full-time job. Consider the fact that whoever watches your child or children is not babysitting. Instead, they are having the privilege of instilling truths, knowledge, principles, and character into your child.

In the years I have served young mothers, I have noted many changes in parenting in America. The most recent is the strong drive of competent, educated women returning home for a season to invest in their children.

Consider this truth found in Psalm 127: Children are a blessing. Children are not our possessions; we do not own them. But we are called to care for and train them.

there's nobody like you

A woman came to speak to me following a keynote message I delivered. Here is her story.

> My lifelong friend—I went to college with her, I was her maid of honor at her wedding, we went through our pregnancies together, and we spent four years being friends and young mothers together—came to ask me if I would watch her two children for

six months so she could return to work to pay off a huge medical expense created by the birth of her then 18-month-old. Without hesitation, I agreed.

There was no one I loved more, and there were no other two children I knew or loved more. As a matter of fact, I often said, "I love your children as I love my own."

The first six weeks of this arrangement went very well. I missed our daily interaction as friends, but I knew this arrangement was temporary, and there was an enormous sense of satisfaction at being able to help in this tangible way. During week number seven, I was doing chores in the kitchen, when I saw the two oldest children, both age four, hand-in-hand, headed straight for the street, and a car was approaching. I ran out the door screaming "Stop!" at the top of my lungs.

I instinctively grabbed for my child first, then her child.

If they had been even two feet farther apart, I would have saved my own child and lost my friend's. I was shocked and forced to admit that instinct had led me to save my child first.

No one can recreate those feelings. I had to acknowledge I was the best choice to raise my own children.

Traci, a mom from Baltimore, capsulized the feelings of a growing number of moms in our country who are choosing not to let their children be raised by relatives, babysitters, or daycare workers: "No one will take care of my baby like I will."

You already know that I'm a cheerleader for moms at home. I respect and admire couples who, through great personal sacrifice and discipline, prayer and perseverance, can make it work while mom stays at home. Stay-at-home moms know that someone has to care for their children, so they are choosing to do it themselves. If you're a mom at home, you've made an excellent choice because no one will take care of your children like you will.

you are unique!

If you're drawn to be a full-time, at-home mom, you have probably identified some of the reasons behind your desire. You believe it will benefit your children—and you're right. Your husband may be encouraging you to stay home, and you want to consider his wishes. Perhaps you believe, as I do, that being an at-home mom will enrich you as a woman of God. I also believe that a husband's career will flourish more when his wife is handling the home and children. For all these reasons, you are right to stay at home.

But there's another reason you should consider, especially if you're still trying to decide if you should make a commitment to stay home. As a mother, you have more influence on the life of your child than anyone else. I've heard that, at one minute old, a baby will turn his head 180 degrees just to look at his mother's face, a face he will prefer above all others. And an infant will respond to his mother's voice—a voice he heard before birth—above all others. Your child has a greater potential for attachment and bonding to you than anyone else. By God's design, you are the primary caregiver and molder of your child. A decision to be an at-home mom is a decision to maximize your impact on your children.

Dr. Jay Belsky, a Pennsylvania State University psychologist who has been researching the effects of infant childcare for 25 years, discovered that a baby forms an attachment with the person who provides his main care, typically his mother, during his first year of life. If the mother responds promptly and in the same manner every time her infant cries for food or comfort, she cultivates what Belsky calls a "secure attachment." The infant trusts the mother and is assured by her predictability and availability. She functions as a "haven of safety" from which the infant can confidently move out and explore his environment.[2]

Attachment Parenting is the philosophy and practice of parenting methods that foster strong, healthy emotional bonds between parents and children in addition to the protection of the infant's physical needs. Attachment Parenting centers on nurturing and securing a trust relationship within the child. In practical terms, a child who is firmly bonded and attached to his parents is sure there will be food to eat, a place to sleep, a regular voice saying the same things repeatedly.

I was 40 years old before I faced the "distrust" system built into me as a child. The ability to trust others was weak and causing relationship difficulties. I accepted the need to change my "trust" patterns with everyone near and dear to me. It was a long and tedious process.

Dr. Armand M. Nicholi, Jr., who has served at Harvard Medical School and Massachusetts General Hospital, has written much about the influence of the mother in family life. His studies indicate that early parental absence—especially the absence of the mother—has a significant negative impact on children. Nicholi concluded:

1. When a child is separated from its mother permanently and not provided adequate substitute care, the infant becomes visibly distressed and is subjected to high risk for both physical and psychological disturbances in development.

2. When a child is separated from its mother unwillingly, even for brief periods of time, the child shows visible distress and when placed in a strange environment and cared for by a succession of strange people, the distress becomes more intense. The reaction follows a typical sequence. The child at first protests vigorously and tries desperately to recover the mother. Later the child seems to despair of recovering her, although he remains preoccupied with her return. Still later, if she does not return, the child seems to lose interest in her and to become emotionally detached from her.[3]

By contrast, in his research on family life, Dr. Nicholi has discovered three common denominators for healthy family life. Notice that all three provide maximum opportunity for a parent's impact in his or her child's life:

1. The parents have a high degree of commitment to the concept of family and a strong commitment to their own family. They give the family the highest priority. The family plays a key role in the way they live their lives.

2. They find time to spend together and know how to spend this time profitably in a way that permits them to be emotionally, as well as physically, accessible to one another.

3. They embrace a philosophy of life that provides a spiritual dimension for the family. Most of these families possess a strong faith that helps bind them together and that provides a resource they can draw on to help cope with crises and adversity.[4]

Dr. Nicholi sums up his report by saying, "We need a radical change in our thinking about family. We need a society where people have the freedom to be whatever they choose—but if they choose to have children, then those children must be given the highest priority."[5]

This observation speaks to moms who make the difficult choice to stay at home and to their husbands who make the equally difficult choice to support their families and be content with what one full-time income provides. If Dr. Nicholi is right, by staying at home you are giving your children the priority and firsthand care they need, enabling your family to be among the most successful in our nation.

Additionally, the child who is more often in an environment that "requires" a certain behavior, is a child who has difficulty knowing what *he* wants. Someone is always telling him what they want from him. The result is adults who often have difficulty making decisions, making choices, and who are frustrated by not having self-knowledge.

A 2005 *Journal of Attachment Parenting, International,* in an article entitled "8 Ideals of Attachment Parentling," listed these tenets:

1. Preparation of Childbirth—Prenatal decisions including kind of birth.

2. Emotional Responsiveness—Lots of nurturing and responding with touch, eye contact, determining needs for food, discomfort, illness and loneliness Soothing the child with rocking, holding, nursing words, songs, verses that communicate you are reliable and dependable.

3. Breastfeeding—Breastfeeding meets baby's need for optimum nutrition and physical contact.

4. Baby Wearing and Nurturing Touch—"Wearing" baby by using soft, cozy carriers.

5. Sharing Sleep—Keeping baby in close proximity in a safe sleeping environment.

6. Avoiding Frequent or Prolonged Separations—Babies have an intense need for physical presence of a loving, response parent.

7. Positive Discipline—Boundaries and limit setting are necessary as children grow.

8. Maintaining Balance in Family Life—Parents need to nurture themselves as well as their children having their own emotional needs meet. This avoids parent burnout.

While you may not agree with all Attachment Parenting International (API) espouses, I'm sure you see the overarching need for "key" attachment.

While Belsky is not a member of API, he confirms that babies who do not form this secure attachment generally are less competent, less cooperative, and less self-controlled as toddlers. As they get older they run a high risk of developing behavior problems.[6]

Sharon France, a leader at a crisis nursery in Phoenix, Arizona, told me an incredible story that illustrates the power of a child's inherent attachment to his mother. Children from homes characterized by physical or sexual abuse are brought to this nursery for protection. They are bathed, fed, comforted, held, read to, and spoken kindly to.

And yet, Sharon said, the moment the abusive mother walks into the room to visit, the child lights up with enthusiasm and excitement. The glow of delight exists despite the fact that the mother causes harm and pain. The child's emotional attachment for his mother, even when she is abusive, is beyond our ability to understand. It reveals the plan of the Father in heaven for the relationship between a child and his mother.

the daycare dilemma

An extensive study by the Urban Institute published in 2000 shows that 48 percent of working families with children under the age of 13 paid for childcare. The average monthly expense was $286 per month, or an average of 9 percent of earnings. For families paying 9 percent of their earnings for childcare, the expense is probably the second largest in the family's budget, after rent or mortgage. Of course, that also means 52 percent of working families do not spend any of their earnings on childcare. The Urban Institute cited another study by the Children's Defense Fund that concluded the high cost of childcare puts quality childcare out of reach for many working families.

Dr. Nicholi's observations are considerably relevant to the recent trend in our society of mothers relegating their children to be raised by outside agencies such as daycare centers while they work. Each week nearly 5 million children are left unsupervised after school. I have talked to some mothers who tearfully agree that daycare is doing more harm than good in their families. Some children are better behaved in the childcare center than they are at home. Some children reach the point where they don't even miss their mothers when they're apart.

For Benay Clark, facing her 2½-year-old daughter, Mallory, before her husband takes her to daycare each morning is a real struggle. Sometimes Mallory clings to her. She says she's scared and she asks why her mother has to have a job. "I've cried on my way to work many times," Benay admits.

Irene Smith, who runs the childcare center where Mallory spends her days, said she often sees tears on parents' as well as children's faces. Mothers and fathers tell her they had a parent at home when they were children, and they wish they could do the same. But they can't because their financial situation requires them to work.[7]

Some parents try to rationalize daycare for infants and toddlers by saying it "socializes" them. But many child development experts say the most important kind of socialization for children this age is the development of a close one-on-one relationship. Some believe this close relationship with a parent helps ensure the ability to develop close relationships in the future, such as marriage. While long-term studies on daycare are not yet conclusive, preliminary indications suggest that children raised in daycare produce fewer successful marriages, fewer nuclear families, and greater incidents of depression.

Recent research shows that while daycare children initially do better academically, children cared for at home are better at recognizing and expressing feelings than daycare children. And home-care children are quick to catch up academically. Furthermore, children who don't begin group care until they are three are dramatically healthier. Many pediatricians say children younger than three are more susceptible to disease.[8]

Researchers Deborah Lowell Vandell and Mary Ann Corasaniti of the University of Texas report that children who are in daycare during preschool years are more likely, by the time they reach third grade, to be uncooperative and unpopular than those raised by full-time mothers. Vandell and Corasaniti discovered that children who had been in full-time childcare programs during preschool years demonstrated poorer study skills, lower grades, and diminished self-concept in later years. Their research suggests that extensive childcare during a child's first year is significantly correlated with retarded social, emotional, and intellectual development.

Megan Rosenfeld reports that children who spend their early years in daycare grow up differently. They are more hyperactive, less responsive to adults, less curious, less altruistic toward other children, and less likely to develop strong one-on-one relationships. And yet hundreds of thousands of school-age children today go from the classroom to an after-school program.[9]

Bryna Siegel, a Stanford University developmental psychologist, spent over a thousand hours observing small children in nonmaternal care. She reports she can go into a preschool and identify the children who have been in long-term daycare just by watching them. They are the children who seek to meet their needs by following rules instead of seeking the help of adults, who are not viewed as resources but as "a sort of controlling gray mass."

On the basis of her research, Siegel now urges women to reexamine their choices about staying at home to raise their children. She asks, "How much of your life is going to be spent as a mother of a little baby? When you are 60 years old, what are you more likely to remember: the first six months of your child's life or a case you won?"[10]

available for bonding

In 2001, Cynthia Langham, at the University of Detroit, released some data about children growing up too fast or in too busy an environment. In it she stated that children of nonavailable parents and alcoholic parents provide the same effects of feeling abandoned or pressured into growing up too fast, when their emotions must develop ahead of their bodies.

Have you ever held a small child for a short period of time? Sure, we all have. As long as the child continues in a happy frame of mind, we continue to hold, talk, and coo. But as soon as the child becomes so unruly we cannot quiet or settle him, what do we do? Yes, we hand him over to his mother. Not to an older woman in the room, not to the father, not to the child psychologist, but to his mother. It's instinctive; she always seems to be the one who knows what to do.

One single mother continued to work long, erratic hours, leaving her children in the care of others. But Carol soon realized that her children needed her more than she needed a job. She said, "If you neglect to take care of your car, it's going to break down. If you don't spend time getting close to your children, something will happen you'll be sorry for."

Carol took a job with better hours so she could devote more time to her family. Her salary suffered as a result of her focus on child-rearing. But the daily rewards of watching her children mature, seeing her daughter in her dance recitals and her son in his wrestling tournaments, more than compensated for any slippage on the career ladder.

Every child attaches himself to and bonds with someone, hopefully his parents. The child who bonds with mother and father is a secure child. As the attachment grows, the child is better behaved, feels safe, loved, and competent, and is able to move forward in his life. The more time you spend with your child, the greater the opportunity for this healthy attachment.

But without sufficient bonding a child will feel insecure, unaccepted, and unloved to some degree. He may be prone to react to things instead of respond to them. Daycare workers or babysitters who come and go only make things worse. The insecurity that arises from insufficient bonding with his parents may plague the child throughout life.

A well-attached, secure baby left for a short time in the care of others is easily comforted by his mother and eager to see her. An insecure baby is not. He is angry about his mother leaving him. When she returns he is still angry. This is what continued exposure to daycare can do. No matter how good the care, nobody can provide the attachment and security your child needs better than you.

If you're beginning to feel guilty about not being more available to bond with your child, that certainly isn't my purpose. However, perhaps it's a good sign. My daughter, Anissa, met a woman attorney who felt so guilty about leaving her child in daycare she cried every day for the first 30 days. I believe Anissa's question to her was a good one: "Why don't you follow your feelings and respond to the guilt by changing your lifestyle?"

Guilt can be a God-given emotion that helps to redirect us. Good guilt, righteous guilt, moral guilt has value. Author Karen Mains says this kind of guilt turns us around and moves us in the right direction.

If you feel guilty about leaving your child in the care of others while you work, if you miss your child when someone else is caring for him or her, and if you feel God tugging at your heart to make yourself more available to bond with your child, give heed to these feelings. They are signposts from God to turn you in the direction He has for you. He may be inviting you to choose an at-home life with your children.

Nancy is an excellent example of an available, at-home mom. Nancy's daughter, Amy, a junior in college, was home for the summer searching for a job. After filling out several applications, Amy left town one Sunday for a quick overnight trip.

But on Monday morning a prospective employer called with a job offer for Amy. Nancy took the call. The job was perfect—good salary, good hours, a great opportunity. "Could your daughter begin today, in two hours?" the employer asked.

"Sure," Nancy answered, realizing Amy wouldn't be home in time. "Is it okay if I take her first shift?"

Nancy worked the first day of Amy's summer job (she also kept her earnings!) because she was committed to being an available at-home mom.

being available looks different daily

Why should you stay at home to raise your children? The statistical evidence indicates the alternatives are not as valuable to your children. But the choice is yours. The power of choice is enormous. Choose well. Choose with sound facts, good counsel, and prayer.

Don't settle for good or better, settle only for the best. Remember, the common begin, and the uncommon finish. Finish strong!

You *are* the best choice!

4

motherhood is a ministry!

Ministry: 1. agent; 2: a high officer of state (home); entrusted with the management of a division; the necessary tactical and administrative services to funtion as a self-contained unit!

The call to motherhood is a unique and individual call. No two mothers do it the same way. Don't concern yourself with someone else's call or how others serve God. Keep focused on how you respond to Romans 12:1: "I urge you therefore, brethren, by the mercies of God, to present your bodies a living and holy sacrifice, acceptable to God, which is your spiritual service of worship."

don't let your ministry get sidetracked

Following nursing school and marriage, Terry did not work outside the home. She served in her church by working with women's groups. Then at age 35 Terry had her first child. She had to step away from all her church responsibilities to care for her new son.

After seven months of full-time mothering, Terry complained, "I feel bad because I don't have a ministry." She was wrong, wasn't she? We often define a ministry as something we do at the church. Sometimes we even view our families as obstacles to "real" ministry. But the ministry of motherhood is more significant than leading a women's group, serving on the Christian education committee, or singing in the choir.

You may never have thought of mothering as a ministry. Those of you who have made the difficult choice to stay at home and raise your children despite all the sacrifices do so because you believe it is the most important thing you can do for your kids. It is also a ministry to God. Don't let anything come between you and your ministry.

The world tells you, "Somebody else can raise your children. You don't have to stay at home. You can raise them to serve Christ on 'quality time.'" Resist those voices. Stay close to the One you serve so that your words, your deeds, your time, and your money reflect your call to be a mom. Your children will benefit from your choice, and Jesus will be pleased.

You may find it difficult to think about serving your heavenly Father when your days are filled with such earthly tasks as changing diapers, cleaning, cooking, chauffeuring, and refereeing kids. So here are several key thoughts that will help you transform every one of your mothering responsibilities into a love offering.

1. *View your ministry to your family as a ministry to Christ.* Imagine that you are meeting Jesus upon your entrance to heaven. He smiles warmly and says, "Welcome, blessed child of My Father. Come and enjoy the kingdom I have prepared for you. For I skinned My knee, and you cleaned and bandaged it. I missed the bus at school, and you came and picked Me up. I was away on a business trip, and you spent most of your weekend typing the proposal I had to turn in at work on Monday."

"Wait a minute, Lord," you might interrupt. "I never bandaged Your knee, picked You up from school, or typed a proposal for You."

And He replies, "Oh, yes you did. Whatever you did in loving ministry to your husband and children, you did to Me." (See Matthew 25:34-40.)

If Christ were here physically, you would be delighted and excited to cook for Him, clean for Him, and care for His needs. When you serve your family, you are serving Christ. As you cook for your family, you cook for Jesus. As you clean up a child's mess, you do it first for Jesus. As you care for the needs of your child's father, you do it for Jesus. We do it all for Him.

My husband, David, is a semi-retired tax lawyer, and I have had the privilege of laundering and ironing his shirts on a weekly basis. It brings me joy because David tells me it's one of the sweet gifts I give him. I love the "bennies" of his kind remarks about my doing his shirts. He knows that I do his shirts with love and care.

As I prepare every shirt I pray for David. I'm excited about making each shirt a pleasing gift to him. That's how we should view every task we must do for our family members—as a gift for Christ.

2. *God's inexhaustible reservoir of love is the resource for your ministry of motherhood.* The enormous measure of love we feel for a brand-new baby is amazing. We see his tiny hands, his great need, his dependency on us, and love pours from our heart. But usually by the time he's two years old, our supply of human love has dipped very low or completely bottomed out!

You will never possess enough human love to stay at home, sacrifice for your children, and raise them the way God directs. You simply don't have that much love. It is God's love that gives you the grace that is sufficient to every challenge of mothering. You need God's love and grace to live sacrificially for your children and point them to Jesus.

You need a good attitude about being at home. My most effective attitude check is found in Psalm 24:3-4: "Who may ascend into the hill of the Lord?...He who has clean hands and a pure heart." To me, "clean hands" represent my actions and "pure heart" stands for my attitude. Yes, there are times when I am disciplined to act without my emotions following. But as a rule I desire to have a pure heart about being at home, not just a "get the job done in 20 years and be free" mentality.

3. *You must rely on God's wisdom and understanding for the ministry of training your children.* German poet and dramatist Goethe said, "We can't form our children on our own concepts. We must take them and love them as God gives them to us."

The verse we parents so often hear is Proverbs 22:6: "Train up a child in the way he should go, even when he is old he will not depart from it." How are we supposed to know the way each child should go? I believe that God can teach mothers what needs to be accomplished in their children and how to train them in that way. He knows you and your children completely. And He will give you ideas, answers, and plans if you ask and listen.

Jacob blessed his 12 sons with a blessing appropriate to each one. How did he know what to say about each child? Jacob understood each one. He knew their needs, their potential, their gifts, and their personality styles. He knew them well enough to bless them individually and appropriately. Study each of your children and rely on God's understanding. Then you'll be able to bless each one through your wise mothering.

4. *You must carry out your ministry in the authority of Christ.* Since motherhood is a ministry for Christ, your mothering must be accomplished in His authority. In fact, one of the definitions of motherhood I found is "a woman in authority." Are you a woman in authority over your children? Do you understand God's authority and where you fit in His line of command?

God holds you and your husband responsible for your children and gives you authority to direct their young lives. Your authority goes beyond giving birth and physically protecting them. You have the authority under God to raise your children to be servants of God. Are you exercising your authority?

5. *Your ministry is to be a servant, not a slave.* I see some mothers who are servants to their children, and I see others who are slaves

to their children. There's a big difference. To serve is to render aid or help. Jesus said, "Whoever wishes to become great among you shall be your servant" (Mark 10:43). If you want to be a great mother, render service to your children by training them in the way they should go.

A slave, however, is in bondage, controlled by a master. Your children should not be your masters. You should not be in bondage to your children. For example, consider the mother at the grocery store with a three-year-old chanting, "I want, I want, I want." Instead of serving the child by giving him what he needs, the mother runs out of patience, and she becomes his slave by giving the little tyrant what he wants.

We all succumb occasionally when our children insist on something and we are in a public place or bound by time constraints. I'm not talking about these exceptions. I'm talking about the standard. Who's in charge in your house—you or your children? Are you determined to serve your children so they will grow to serve Christ? Or are you the slave who is in bondage to doing whatever your children want in order to keep them from disruptive noises or temper tantrums?

A servant makes sacrifices, offering something precious to God. We make sacrifices, suffer personal losses, and give up things that are valuable to us on behalf of the children we serve. Our sacrifice is patterned after the sacrifice of Christ on the cross, who served our deepest needs by giving His life. As mothers we learn to lay down our lives for our kids on a daily basis, not because our children are in charge, but because we have a vision and a goal of helping them understand the importance of serving Christ. We must choose to be servants, not slaves.

As you think about your day-to-day ministry to your children, realize your possibilities and your limitations. Despite being with them day in and day out, there are some things you can't do for your kids. Allow the following statements from Barbara Johnson on the next two pages to help you understand where you must be responsible and where you must trust God for your child's development.

I gave you life,
but I cannot live it for you.

I can teach you things,
but I cannot make you learn.

I can give you directions,
but I cannot always be there to lead you.

I can allow you freedom,
but I cannot account for it.

I can take you to church,
but I cannot make you believe.

I can teach you right from wrong,
but I can't always decide for you.

I can buy you beautiful clothes,
but I cannot make you lovely inside.

I can offer you advice,
but I cannot accept it for you.

I can give you love,
but I cannot force it upon you.

I can teach you to be a friend,
but I cannot make you one.

I can teach you to share,
but I cannot make you unselfish.

I can teach you respect,
but I can't force you to show honor.

I can grieve about your report card,
but I cannot doubt your teachers.

I can advise you about your friends,
but I cannot choose them for you.

I can teach you about sex,
but I cannot keep you pure.

I can tell you the facts of life,
but I can't build your reputation.

I can tell you about drink,
but I can't say no for you.

I can warn you about drugs,
but I can't prevent you from using them.

I can tell you about lofty goals,
but I can't achieve them for you.

I can let you babysit,
but I can't be responsible for your actions.

I can teach you kindness,
but I can't force you to be gracious.

I can warn you about sins,
but I cannot make your morals.

I can love you as a daughter [or son]
but I cannot place you in God's family.

I can pray for you,
but I cannot make you walk with God.

I can teach you about Jesus,
but I cannot make Him your Savior.

I can teach you to obey,
but I cannot make Jesus your Lord.

I can tell you how to live,
but I cannot give you eternal life.[1]

first things first

The Tyranny of the Urgent by Charles Hummel is well worth your examination. Mr. Hummel tells us that our priorities often get jumbled. We desire to do important things, but we often get sidetracked by urgent things. For example, it is important for moms to raise their children so they will become men and women of integrity and good character so they will choose wisdom. But often our intent gives way to seemingly urgent tasks. The children need to eat, to wear clean clothes, to get to school on time, to get to soccer practice or music lessons, and so on.

Mr. Hummel encourages us to wait for direction from the Lord to keep our priorities straight. It is the Lord who frees us from the tyranny of the urgent. He will help us undertake the important things in our ministry as moms while we deal with, but are not diverted by, the inevitable urgent things.

If you struggle at all with setting priorities and keeping the vision of your ministry clearly before you, I offer you a very simple phrase: The most important ministry is to love Christ. (See chapter 9, "checking your id.") In your heart, tell yourself over and over again that you must reflect Jesus first. Ask yourself often, "Am I setting my roles of wife and mother over my chosen role of follower of Christ?" "Unless the LORD builds the house, they labor in vain who build it" (Psalm 127:1). Your efforts to minister to your children will be feeble if you're not serving the Lord first. Train your thoughts to run to Him first. Recognize and revel in God's character in you and that you are passing it on to your children:

- Pray for your children first each day. Make church attendance together a primary activity of your week.

- Talk enthusiastically about the coming Sunday service and learning experiences with your children just as the Jews in Israel excitedly look forward to every Sabbath. On this point I recommend a wonderful book by Karen Mains, *Keeping Sunday*

Special. It will help your family anticipate, prepare for, and enjoy Sunday church attendance.

- Read to your children about Jesus first. If you bend down to pick up a Walt Disney or Mother Goose storybook, ask yourself, "Have I read to them something about Jesus today? Have I talked to them about Jesus today?" Perhaps as you wake your children in the morning you should read to them from the Bible or from a Bible storybook. It will help them learn early that His mercies are new every morning (see Lamentations 3:22-23). Read, read, read to your children!

The do-it-first principle applies to many things you do with your children. For example, your family is probably accustomed to talking to God first when you sit down at the dinner table. But what about when you sit down to watch TV? Do you consider watching a Christian video first or praying together about what you are about to watch?

I don't intend to be legalistic about it, but the do-it-first principle was a tool that helped me focus on the important things in my life and act on my priorities. Reminding myself to "do it first" helped me put Christ first and value what He values. This practice of doing it first will become a habit and lifestyle, not a rigid rule, as this story illustrates.

> A young boy came to the pastor of his church and said, "Even though I'm young, I want to do something for the King."
>
> The pastor was perplexed about the boy's request. He wanted to encourage the willing lad, but the boy was too young to teach a class or sing in the choir. What could he do?
>
> After a few days of thought, the pastor had a great idea. He called the boy in and told him that he could serve the King by ringing the church bell. The pastor explained that he wanted the boy to come to the church four times a day, climb the bell tower, and ring the bell.
>
> The boy was thrilled. He had found a way to serve the King. He joyously set about his daily task. For months on end he climbed the tower and rang the bell four times every day without fail.
>
> But one day he arrived at the church to find it locked and

boarded up. He thought the men of the church must be doing some repairs and forgot to tell him. But his service to the King was to ring the bell on schedule. So he carefully wriggled between some boards, climbed the tower, and rang the bell.

When he came out he found two groups of people on the sidewalk in front of the church. They were arguing with each other noisily. "No one is supposed to use this building. Who rang the bell?" a man shouted.

"I rang the bell, sir," the boy interrupted timidly.

"Young man, we have dismissed the pastor and closed the church because of a doctrinal dispute," the man huffed. "Why did you ring the church bell?"

The boy thought for a moment. Then he said, "Well, I'm sorry the pastor's gone, and I'm sorry you're not getting along. But I ring the bell to serve the King. Ringing the bell is my ministry."

Don't be daunted by the word "minister." It simply means one who served. Many countries around the world call their senior leaders "ministers," such as Minister of the Treasury. Like this young boy and leaders in the world, you can handle a lot if your ultimate goal is to serve God. And as an at-home mom, your ministry is motherhood. You are the only one God has called to mother your children. Did you know that in Hebrew, the word "mother" means "bond of the family"? God has chosen you to bind your family together. How important it is that you faithfully and joyfully do the job God has called you to do, keeping your eyes on Him and not on others.

A first among firsts in the ministry of a believing mom is taking that big step of commitment; saying the "Big Yes" to being a stay-at-home mom. Let's consider the significance of that one little word, "Yes!"

saying the "big yes" to being an at-home mom

Desire to be with your children 24/7.

Ever notice how easy it is to say yes? Somehow yes is easier to pronounce than no, and it's usually more fun! Yes is a little word with big consequences. *Yes,* I'll marry you. *Yes,* I want to have a baby. *Yes,* I'll live anywhere in the world with you. *Yes,* I'll serve the Lord.

Remember the day, the night, the hour, the place when he asked you, "Will you marry me?" You were waiting for that question, hoping for that question. For days—maybe for years—you daydreamed about how he would ask you, how you would feel when he asked you, and what your response would be. Was that an easy yes to say? For most of us it was very easy to say yes to the men we loved and who proposed to us. We felt we could have climbed to the mountaintop and shouted, "Yes, yes, yes!" for all the world to hear.

Saying yes to being an at-home mom is one of those big yeses. It's usually easy to say the first yes. Your heart is full of determination. Your wee one holding your finger tightly fills you with emotion. You are motivated, and you probably have family members who are ready to support you in your decision. Your hormones say everything will be rosy. You know it will be a challenge and a sacrifice, but it seems so right. So you pause, take a deep breath, and say it: Yes!

Then reality hits, and saying yes to staying at home is followed by years of small yeses, just as the big yes to your man's proposal was followed by years of saying yes to nightly dinners cooked by you, changing your name, housecleaning, laundry, etc. Your fruitfulness as an at-home mom results from your commitment to say yes again and again to the many mundane tasks that will automatically follow your big yes to stay at home. Yes, I'll take the 2 AM feeding. Yes, I'll do the laundry. Yes to a human bundle of boundless energy who doesn't give me a moment to myself. Yes to carpooling and seemingly endless hours at the soccer, baseball, or football field. Yes to getting up early or staying up late just to study God's Word and pray. Yes, yes, yes.

If you have already decided to stay at home, or you are on the verge of saying yes, realize that it will only work when you are totally committed to the millions of small yeses that follow. These follow-through yeses are the measure of an at-home mom.

Perhaps you're still at the stage of wanting to stay at home, but you haven't said the big yes yet. You may feel nudges in this direction, and you're hoping something in these pages will give you the courage to say yes. Perhaps the following words, written by an unknown author will encourage you.

> Oh my child, be quick to obey the moving of My Spirit. My ways may seem diametrically opposed to reason, but obey Me regardless of the cost. You will in every case be amply repaid for any sacrifice by an abundance of blessing. The more difficult the assignment, the more lavish the reward. Stay pliable in My hand. Don't resist Me or be unaware of My working. Don't question what I am making of you. Trust Me and give Me a free hand. You will be surprised and full of joy when the end is revealed.

a time of transition

What can you expect after you say the big yes to staying at home full time? You can expect a period of transition—possibly a difficult one—especially if you are stepping out of a job and career. Your feelings may become a bit jumbled—glad to be at home one day, wishing you were back at work the next. You are giving up a paycheck and everything it can buy. That paycheck is a form of validation you lose completely. The transition away from job and earnings requires a lot of prayer and commitment on your part.

If you are moving from two incomes to one in this transition, you are saying goodbye to some of your discretionary income. For some women, even a small amount of "mad money" is a sign of freedom: freedom to escape to a movie, get a new outfit, buy some makeup. But when you give up your job, you may also forfeit many of your financial perks.

A survey released by the compensation expert firm Salary.com concluded that stay-at-home moms perform a variety of jobs that, if totaled, would pay $134,121 a year.[1] That news report became the number one story e-mailed on Yahoo!

However, there is a paycheck for being an at-home mom. But it comes sporadically and in surprising ways: a loving, appreciative glance from your husband, an unexpected hug from your child, the joy of watching his first step, the handmade gifts. The wonderful thing about these rewards is that there's no withholding tax. You get to keep the full amount. You'll want to deposit these personal paychecks in your memory bank so you can withdraw them when times get tough. The dividends are terrific!

There's more to the transition than just a change in your employment and financial status. Staying at home is a period of continual adjustment as you face new situations, many of them happening simultaneously.

You'll notice a change in your independence. When you became a parent you discovered how much of your personal time, energy, and resources were required by your tiny infant. In transitioning from part-time or full-time working mom to full-time at-home mom you will lose another measure of independence. The more of yourself you make available, the more your children seem to require.

Some of the other changes are pretty obvious. Your daily schedule will look different (did I say schedule?). What you wear will look different as you go from suits and high heels to sweats and tennies. Your level of intellectual stimulation will change. You no longer have the daily resource of adult coworkers or clients to interact with. The challenge of solving business problems and accomplishing corporate goals is replaced by the challenge of resolving conflicts over who gets to play with a favorite toy. Your vocabulary will also be simplified (some days it will consist of a single word—no!).

As you recognize and accept the changes that come with your commitment to stay at home, do three things.

- *Lament your losses.* Be honest with yourself about how you feel about the losses that come with the big yes. Cherish your past, but don't cling to it. Don't ignore the fact that some things are lost forever.

- *Grieve the separation.* Anytime we suffer a major upheaval in our lives we experience a grieving period. Accept that period, seek counsel, and be prepared to grieve. Studies about transitions indicate from ending one thing to beginning and understanding what you are now doing takes about two years!

- *Rejoice over what is praiseworthy.* Rejoice over what you have gained in your decision: new challenges, the opportunity to impact your family in new and more meaningful ways, freedom from stressful job situations. Rejoice as bills get paid. Rejoice as the kids grow physically and spiritually. Take time to count the blessings of God and verbalize your gratefulness to Him.

Also be mindful of your husband and the effect your transition time has on him, an effect that is easy to overlook. His life is also being altered, though not as dramatically as yours. Don't expect him to understand everything that is happening inside you during this big change in your life. He is not a mind-reader. He has not walked the road of transition from work to home as you have.

Talk to him about your feelings, about the loss of your freedoms, about the lack of spending money. Trust his counsel; he knows you well. Sharing your insights and concerns will help deepen his knowledge of you. Do your best to describe to him the task of mothering, how demanding it is, and how it affects your energy level. Assure him as you assure yourself that the sacrifice is worth it and that the problems you encounter are for a season, not a lifetime.

Remember that your husband is a provision from the Lord's hand. Your mate's commitment to hard work is one of the reasons you can be an at-home mom. You are a team and in agreement. Relish this fact.

a time to stand firm

In addition to the difficulties of the transition, you can expect criticism for being an at-home mom. The criticism will come from people who believe that mothering is not particularly valuable and that your children can be raised by anyone.

You can expect criticism from peers who believe you are wasting your education and skills. Your former boss may expect you to return to your job and criticize you for deciding not to. He or she may believe that mothers don't need to be the primary caregivers for their children.

You can also expect some people to be frustrated with you. They can't believe your decision to stay at home. The question most often asked at-home moms by frustrated, misunderstanding friends and former colleagues is "What do you do all day?" You may have asked the same question before you felt directed to stay at home. The stereotype of the fat, slovenly, mindless homemaker continues to circulate even though it is far from accurate. Be ready for the people who will cast you in that role.

Most of us have difficulty going against the tide of popular opinion and dealing with the criticism that results. It's hard to stand alone (at least you think you're standing alone). That's why you must look to God for support. You also need support and encouragement from other moms who believe and act as you do. (We'll discuss more about the supportive sisterhood of at-home moms in chapter 19.)

Once you have made your decision to be at home, be prepared to stand firm against the criticism. As Thomas Jefferson said, "In matters of fashion and culture, flow with the current, but in matters of principle, stand like a rock in the torrent."

There was a strong, negative reaction in an audience of young seminary women when the speaker suggested that the students might find the work of a nanny rewarding. Then one woman stood and quieted the group by reminding them that Aristotle was a nanny to Alexander the Great.

Your child may not be the next Alexander the Great, but the task of raising him and molding his life should not be taken lightly. There is no need to defend the choice you and your husband have made. If God has called you to the ministry of an at-home mom, you need offer no other explanations.

Your satisfaction will begin to set in when you say that first big yes by totally committing yourself to stay at home. Your goals suddenly become clear:

- to grow as an individual
- to love your husband
- to raise your children
- to make your home a place of warmth and restoration for all who enter.

Be strong and keep your eye on your goals. You will succeed. By saying yes to your children, you contribute to the building of your city, state, and country. Thank you!

6

cultivating character in your children

Happy will that house be in which
relations are formed from character.
EMERSON

What are the traits of good character? Self-discipline, compassion, responsibility, friendship, work, courage, perseverance, honesty, loyalty, and faith.

In your enthusiasm to protect and nurture your children, don't forget to teach your children what character looks like. Celebrate character. Let your children know that character matters in your family. Character issues happen moment by moment, hour by hour, day by day. When we least expect the need for character it jumps out, requiring a choice.

One message on one of Dr. James Dobson's call-in Valentine radio programs was from a grateful husband, Chris, to his wife, Jennifer, a stay-at-home mom. I cried when I heard it:

> I know you struggle with being a stay-at-home mom and the little bit of recognition the world gives to that occupation. I know

the days get long sometimes, and I know that conversations with a two-year-old can be slightly lacking in intellectual stimulation.

I've tried to tell you how much it means to me knowing that our little girl is with you each day...The work you are doing is the most important of all. You have a little person in your hands, a little person who hungers for something she cannot identify yet. Now where is that little person going to learn that that something is Jesus Christ if she doesn't have a mommy like you to show her?

I thank God each day that He made you my wife. One of the reasons I thank Him is because of our little girl, who has such confidence, such joy, such an exuberant spirit because of the love of her mother.[1]

Remember, home is a child's first church, seminary, Bible study, and educational classroom.

Tim Kimmel's book *Raising Kids for True Greatness* describes what he calls success traps in our culture and God's definition of true greatness found in the truths of Scripture:

"Success Traps"	God's Plan for Greatness
Wealth	Humility
Beauty	Gratefulness
Power	Generosity
Fame	Servant spirit

Francis Schaeffer, founder of L'Abri in Switzerland and a noted philosopher, is quoted as saying, "The spirit of the age [culture] seeps into the church [us]." Kimmel addresses this seeping process and reminds us that raising children God's way is the best. So look for warning signs that you need to refocus your parenting. For instance, generally spending more time and energy in the culture's design for your children versus God's design. Here are a few specifics:

1. Educations that will bring high salaries vs. following God's built-in bent of your child.

2. Emphasis on external appearance with too much exercise and

fashion investment vs. a balance of body care and soul care.

3. The need to be the "leader," "president," or "top of activities and events" vs. a clear understanding of roles in life.

4. Ability to honor and allow someone to have the upfront jobs, the limelight vs. the ability to serve others.

are babies sinners?

When a brand-new mother comes to me seeking counsel or direction regarding her stay-at-home decision, I gently say to her, "This wee, precious child you're holding is a sinner." The mother often grimaces with inner pain and pulls away from me. She wonders how I can possibly say such a hard thing.

It is harsh, isn't it? But it's true. Your children are sinners who must be led to the Savior. They must choose to make the God of the universe the Lord of their lives. And as their mom, you are God's primary instrument for helping them make this decision. The sooner you acknowledge your child's sinful state, the sooner you can begin to center on bringing him or her to Jesus.

This is the governing principle behind a Christian mother who stays at home. Mothers and fathers are an important part of God's strategy for propagating the faith and redeeming people for Himself. As an at-home mom, you may have wonderful opportunities to witness to your neighbors, the members of your coffee klatch, and the clerks in the market. But in your zeal to share Christ with others, don't overlook the potential disciples in your own family. The possibilities for enlarging the kingdom of God within the walls of your home are very exciting.

I challenge you, I admonish you, I encourage you to recognize that the children God has given you are sinners who must be pointed to the Savior. Make it your goal to tell your children about Jesus so they can make a decision for Him. Start cultivating character early. Babies can understand much more than we typically believe. Studies indicate that from a rudimentary understanding of math to a sense of past and future, children under one year know a lot more than they are saying. Remember this when you speak, read, and interface with your infants. If they could talk they would surprise you.

Don't make it a priority to raise beauty queens, brilliant scholars, successful career persons, or wealthy entrepreneurs. Lead them first to be lovers of Jesus. I guarantee that children who grow up to love Jesus because of your ministry will bless you as their mother (see Proverbs 31:28).

Your primary ministry as a mom is to point these sinners to Christ. Give them everything they will need to make the decision for Christ. Teach them character in word and deed. Show them Christ's character found in the truth of Scripture. The following list will provide you with simple definitions and a biblical reference for character traits. Use it as a baseline for your child training.

You might like to begin your training with a review of Psalm 15, often referred to as the Christian Constitution because it is riddled with character traits.

Character Traits to Instill in Your Children
(Scripture references are from the English Standard Version)

Attentive—Mindful of the comfort of others: "...look not only to his own interests, but also to the interest of others" (Philippians 2:4).

At-one-ment—Satisfied not ambitious: "...be content with what you have" (Hebrews 13:5).

Authentic—the real thing: "...delight in truth in the inward being" (Psalm 51:6).

Cheerful—In good spirits; merry heart: "A joyful heart is good medicine..." (Proverbs 17:22).

Courageous—Bold, confident: "Be strong and courageous..." (Joshua 1:6).

Forgiving—Easily gives up resentment: "...forgiving each other; as the Lord has forgiven you" (Colossians 3:13-14).

Generous—Easily gives to others: "...God loves a cheerful giver" (2 Corinthians 9:6-15).

Gracious—Kind and full of grace: "...the Lord is gracious" (Psalm 111:4); "...grace and truth came through Jesus Christ" (John 1:17).

Hospitality—Offered from your eyes, hand, and heart anywhere: "Show hospitality to one another without grumbling" (1 Peter 4:9).

Humility—Able to put self aside: "...walk humbly with your God" (Micah 6:6-8).

Loving and Loveable—I still prefer Nat King Cole's definition: "The greatest thing you'll ever learn is to love and be loved in return"; see John 3:16.

Merciful—Extending compassion: "Render true judgments, show kindness and mercy to one another" (Zechariah 7:9); "...mercy triumphs over judgment" (James 2:13).

Modest—Doesn't need attention; decent in lifestyle and dress: "Adorn themselves in respectable apparel, with modesty and self control, not with braided hair and gold or pearls or costly attire" (1 Timothy 2:9).

Orderly—A way of life (systems) that create calm: "...rejoicing to see your good order and the firmness of your faith in Christ" (Colossians 2:5).

Persevere—Continuing and not quitting: "...keep alert with all perseverance" (Ephesians 6:18).

Prayerful—Communion with God: "...devoting themselves to prayer" (Acts 1:14).

Respectful—Honoring: "Honor everyone" (1 Peter 2:17).

Self-Restraint—Holding oneself in check: "...for God gave us a spirit not of fear but of power and love and self-control (2 Timothy 1:7).

Submissive—Yielded: "...submitting to one another out of reverence for Christ" (Ephesians 5:21).

Steadfast—Firm, fixed and immovable: "Therefore, my beloved brothers, be steadfast, immovable, always abounding in the work of the Lord, knowing that in the Lord your labor is not in vain" (1 Corinthians 15:58).

Truthful—Ability to acknowledge God's truth in all situations: "...speak the truth to one another..." (Zechariah 8:16).

Thankful—A heart of gratitude: "Oh give thanks to the Lord..." (1 Chronicles 16:8).

Teachable—Being willing to be taught: See Acts 18:24-26.

Team Member—Ability to trust others: See Ephesians 5:21.

Tender—Easily broken: "The sacrifices of God are a broken spirit; a broken and contrite heart" (Psalm 51:17).

Wise—Discerning right from wrong: See Hebrews 5:12-14.

Worker—Knowing God planned for man to participate in caring for themselves and others: "...and to work with your hands" (1 Thessalonians 4:11).

an inspiring example

"How do I accomplish the difficult task of preparing my children to be followers of Jesus?" you ask. Primarily through the impact and influence of your life. As adults, we look for a variety of significant ways to influence others and alter the course of their lives for the better. Schoolteachers try to influence their students, pastors try to influence their congregations, and judges try to influence those who stand before them. I believe that mothers have an even greater opportunity to impact their children.

One way to influence your children is by teaching them about God and His Word. In Psalm 78:5-7 we see the importance of teaching our children:

> For He established a testimony in Jacob, and appointed a law in Israel, which He commanded our fathers, that they should teach them to their children; that the generation to come, even the children yet to be born, that they may arise and tell them to their children, that they should put their confidence in God, and not forget the works of God, but keep His commandments.

Deuteronomy 6:5-9 underscores this concern:

> You shall love the Lord your God with all your heart and with all your soul and with all your might. And these words, which I am commanding you today, shall be on your heart; and you shall teach them diligently to your sons and shall talk of them when you sit in your house and when you walk by the way and when you lie down and when you rise up. And you shall bind them as a sign on your hand and they shall be as frontals on your forehead. And you shall write them on the doorposts of your house and on your gates.

As important as teaching is, the "caught it" method of influencing your children is even more effective than the "taught it" method. No matter what you say about Christ, your children will learn more about Him from you as they catch your contagious spirit for serving Him. In everything we do we should be leading them to Christ.

Chuck Swindoll defines leadership as "inspiring influence." As the number one leader in your children's lives, you have an incredible influence on them. What kind of leader are you? In my desk area, I have the phrase, "Enthusiasm is contagious!" How contagious is your enthusiasm for Jesus? Is it making your kids want to serve Him too?

For years I thought I was not a creative person. As a matter of fact, I often said, "I'm not the creative type." But, as Elisabeth Elliot Gren reminded me, "Of course you're creative. The one and only Creator God made you in His image." We are to be imitators of Him. And in doing so, we become inspiring examples for our children to follow.

In God's Word, Christ told us about Himself. In doing so He gave us much to imitate. In His Word there are many others who set good examples. The apostle Paul even admonished us to live as he lived (1 Corintians 11:1). Read God's Word looking for others who were like Christ that you can emulate.

As you seek to know Christ better, you will begin to be like Him as you minister to your family. As you learn to sacrifice and suffer loss, as you learn to set aside your personal desires, as you are willing to pray for your children and put them first, they will see what it means to serve Christ. They will see the invisible Christ in your visible example.

Marc Chagall, one of the world's most famous artists, created 12 stained-glass windows for the Hadassah Hebrew Medical Center in an elevated section of Jerusalem. Each window depicts one of the 12 tribes of Israel. When the sunlight filters through these prominently elevated windows, they glow brilliantly and can be seen around Jerusalem for miles.

You are like one of those stained-glass windows. You have prominence. You have been elevated. You are a mother! As you allow the light of Jesus Christ to filter through you, your children will see His beauty in you. As they are drawn to Him, you will be instrumental in your children's life choices.

affirming character development

Shape your children by focusing on their character traits. When you see them exhibit traits such as faith, integrity, self-discipline, perseverance, and courage, applaud them. Be a role model of exemplary character before them. Identify and promote other role models in their lives who display these qualities. Impress upon your children this thought: Reputation is who people think you are; character is who you are when no one is looking.

Here are two ideas for influencing your children to build positive character traits.

put in a good word

Your words can either tear down or build up your children. Here are a bunch of great ways to tell your children they are loved.

You'll always be tops in my book.

You're so much fun!

You get better at that every time.

Way to go!

Brilliant!

Perfect!

That's great!

That's the best I've ever seen.

You are so thoughtful.

This is a tremendous improvement.

Good for you.

You're such a joy to me.

I really enjoy your smile.

Can Dad put this on the bulletin board at his office?

You handled that beautifully.

You're really special to me.

I enjoy being with you.

That's worth a trophy!

Excellent!

Terrific!

You're so helpful.

Thank you.

I wish I could have done it that well.

I'm impressed.

I know you worked very hard on that.

You're the best.

I love to hear you laugh.

You never cease to amaze me.

Sensational!

I believe in you.

You sure are growing up.

You make me so happy.

I love you.

praying for your children

In 1833, John Abbott wrote: "The efforts which a mother makes for the improvement of her child in knowledge and virtue are necessarily retired and unobtrusive. The world knows not of them; and hence, the world has been slow to perceive how powerful and extensive is this secret and silent influence."

This statement is true of many of the important things you do that go unnoticed in serving your children. But it is especially true of your behind-the-scenes ministry of praying for your children. Perhaps no one but God and your husband knows how much time you spend praying for your kids. But this ministry is vital. Let's face it: Without prayer, anything else you do to influence your children for Jesus is feeble at best.

I'm sure you pray for your children; what mother doesn't? If you need some help with specific topics for prayer, consider praying through the following categories given to me by a friend:

1. *Pray that your children will fear the Lord and serve Him:* "You shall fear only the LORD your God; and you shall worship Him, and swear by His name" (Deuteronomy 6:13).

2. *Pray that your children will know Christ as Savior early in life:* "O God, Thou art my God; I shall seek Thee earnestly; my soul thirsts for Thee, my flesh yearns for Thee, in a dry and weary land where there is no water" (Psalm 63:1).

3. *Pray that your children will hate sin:* "Hate evil, you who love the

LORD, who preserves the souls of His godly ones; He delivers them from the hand of the wicked" (Psalm 97:10).

4. *Pray that your children will be caught when they're guilty:* "It is good for me that I was afflicted, that I may learn Thy statutes" (Psalm 119:71).

5. *Pray that your children will have a responsible attitude in all their interpersonal relationships:* "Then this Daniel began distinguishing himself among the commissioners and satraps because he possessed an extraordinary spirit, and the king planned to appoint him over the entire kingdom" (Daniel 6:3).

6. *Pray that your children will respect those in authority over them:* "Let every person be in subjection to the governing authorities. For there is no authority except from God, and those which exist are established by God" (Romans 13:1).

7. *Pray that your children will desire the right kind of friends and be protected from the wrong kind:* "My son, if sinners entice you, do not consent...Do not walk in the way with them. Keep your feet from their path" (Proverbs 1:10,15).

8. *Pray that your children will be kept from the wrong mate and saved for the right one:* "Do not be bound together with unbelievers; for what partnership have righteousness and lawlessness, or what fellowship has light with darkness?" (2 Corinthians 6:14).

9. *Pray that your children and their prospective mates will be kept pure until marriage:* "Flee immorality...Do you not know that your body is a temple of the Holy Spirit who is in you, whom you have from God, and that you are not your own? For you have been bought with a price: therefore glorify God in your body" (1 Corinthians 6:18-20).

10. *Pray that your children will learn to submit totally to God and actively resist Satan in all circumstances:* "Submit therefore to God. Resist the devil and he will flee from you" (James 4:7).

11. *Pray that your children will be single-hearted, willing to be sold*

out to Jesus: "I urge you therefore, brethren, by the mercies of God, to present your bodies a living and holy sacrifice, acceptable to God, which is your spiritual service of worship. And do not be conformed to this world, but be transformed by the renewing of your mind, that you may prove what the will of God is, that which is good and acceptable and perfect" (Romans 12:1-2).

12. *Pray that your children will be hedged in so the wrong people cannot find their way to them:* "Therefore, behold, I will hedge up her way with thorns, and I will build a wall against her so that she cannot find her paths. And she will pursue her lovers, but she will not overtake them; and she will seek them, but will not find them" (Hosea 2:6-7).

13. *Pray that your children will have quick, repentant hearts:* "Be gracious to me, O God, according to Thy lovingkindness; according to the greatness of Thy compassion blot out my transgressions. Wash me thoroughly from my iniquity, and cleanse me from my sin. For I know my transgressions, and my sin is ever before me" (Psalm 51:1-3).

14. *Pray that your children will honor you and their father so all will go well with them:* "Children, obey your parents in the Lord, for this is right. Honor your father and mother (which is the first commandment with a promise), that it may be well with you, and that you may live long on the earth" (Ephesians 6:1-3).

15. *Pray that your children will be teachable and able to take correction:* "And all your sons will be taught of the LORD; and the well-being of your sons will be great" (Isaiah 54:13); "a wise son accepts his father's discipline, but a scoffer does not listen to rebuke" (Proverbs 13:1).

16. *Pray that your children's lives will bear the fruit of the Spirit:* "The fruit of the Spirit is love, joy, peace, patience, kindness, goodness, faithfulness, gentleness, self-control; against such things there is no law" (Galatians 5:22-23).

17. *Pray that your children will live by the Spirit and not gratify their flesh:* "Walk by the Spirit, and you will not carry out the desire of the flesh" (Galatians 5:16).

18. *Pray that your children will trust in the Lord for direction in their lives, including their occupations:* "Trust in the LORD with all your heart, and do not lean on your own understanding. In all your ways acknowledge Him, and He will make your paths straight" (Proverbs 3:5-6).

Many years ago I discovered that I could pray someone else's prayers, such as prayers from the Bible or prayers written by saints before me. This fact inspired me to write a prayer about Anissa covering specific areas and using certain phrases and some Scripture. I prayed that prayer over and over. Through the years I used this method to help me stay focused and persevere in my prayers. I still do it.

Evelyn is a dear friend who has given me wisdom and insight for reaching into the heart of my child at every age in life. She is the mother of three adult children (and grandmother of four) who are all married and making great choices. Evelyn once told me, "The only assurance I have of access to my children's hearts is through prayer and the power of the Holy Spirit."

In the 175,200 hours you'll spend in the first 20 years of your children's lives, the hours of prayer and cultivating character will be the most important. To further help you set aside time to pray, I've included a prayer calendar my friend Dr. Sandra Wilson and I created that you can photocopy for your personal use.

DAILY PRAYER FOR OUR CHILDREN

Sunday	Monday	Tuesday	Wednesday	Thursday	Friday	Saturday
PSALM 91:11 Lord, I ask Your angels to guard and protect my children today and every day.	**ROMANS 13:13** Father, be with my children to help them behave in my absence.	**MARK 10:16** Jesus, bless my children; may they turn to You for truth.	**JOSHUA 24:15** Dearest God, help my children choose to serve You in their actions and words.	**ACTS 23:11** Lord, give my children courage to do what is right in Your eyes.	**PROVERBS 3:12** Heavenly Father, help my children accept discipline and reap its rewards.	**2 TIMOTHY 2:22** Lord, protect my children from evil and help them flee from evil desires.
DEUTERONOMY 11:13 I pray my children will be faithful to Your commandments.	**1 TIMOTHY 5:4** Jesus, show my children that honoring their own family is pleasing to God.	**PROVERBS 1:3** Lord, guide my children to do what is right and just and fair.	**PHILIPPIANS 4:5** I pray that gentleness will be in my children's hearts as it reflects Your Spirit.	**PROVERBS 4:13** Lord, I pray my children hold on to Your instruction and show wisdom.	**PROVERBS 10:9** Father God, help my children walk with integrity.	**PROVERBS 10:28** Heavenly Father, help my children recognize that a righteous life brings joy.
ROMANS 12:10 Lord, I pray my children honor others in actions, words and deeds.	**PROVERBS 17:22** God, bless my children with a joyful heart.	**1 TIMOTHY 6:17** Help my children put their hopes in You, Lord, as You will provide all.	**PROVERBS 11:17** Jesus, teach my children that being kind to others will reap kindness to them.	**COLOSSIANS 3:8** I pray my children will use appropriate words that are pleasing to You.	**JOHN 15:17** I pray love is abundant in my children.	**PSALM 145:45** Lord, open my children's eyes to Your majesty.
MATTHEW 6:8 God who provides, may my children differentiate between needs and wants.	**1 PETER 2:17** I pray, Father, that my children will show the proper respect to everyone.	**TITUS 2:6-8** I pray my children are encouraged to do good and will to show self-control.	**EPHESIANS 6:1** I pray my children will obey us, as parents, so they will enjoy a long life.	**1 THES. 5:14** I pray my children will help the weak and show patience to everyone.	**1 THES. 4:11-12** Lord, may my children live a quiet life, earning the respect of outsiders.	**2 CORINTHIANS 10:5** Help my children take captive every thought to make it obedient to Christ.
PSALM 100:4 Lord, I pray my children are thankful for all You have done.	**PROVERBS 12:22** Lord, keep my children in truth.	**PSALM 119:104** Lord, give my children supernatural understanding of Your Word.	**COLOSSIANS 3:13** Lord, I pray my children have a forgiving spirit.	**PSALM 90:12** Father, give my children a heart of wisdom.	**1 TIMOTHY 4:12** I pray, Lord, for my children to be an example to others.	**2 CORINTHIANS 6:14** Bless my children's friends, bring them into Your fold, Jesus.

7

your children, loud
and lovable

*It takes an enormous amount of time
to raise a child...The joy of being an
at-home mom is that you are available to
give them the time they need.*

There has been a debate in recent years over whether quality time can substitute for quantity time with our children. In her article "The Myth of Quality Time," Prudence McIntosh reveals a similar discovery:

When William, my youngest, entered the first grade, I spent the first days of my liberation perusing the ragged spiral notebooks and hardback journals in which I had sporadically recorded the past 13 years. I was searching for "quality time." Instead, I found a disorderly kaleidoscope tale of high hopes, rocking chairs, runny noses, loose diapers, loose teeth, Oz books, earaches, music lessons, chicken pox, nightmares, tough talks, interrupted sleep, chalk rocks, spear grass, broken windowpanes, hamster funerals, convulsive laughter, and utterly irrational behavior by both adults and children. Quality time at our house was a relative matter.[1]

It takes an enormous amount of time to raise a child. They need quiet time, play time, and time just to be with you. The joy of being an at-home mom is that you are available to give them the time they need. You are available to be the woman of God in their lives! God tells kids what to do most often through their parents. With all the seminars, books, and tapes available today emphasizing parenting skills and techniques, don't lose sight of the fact that just living with your children day in and day out is one of the most important things you can do for them. A predictable, secure, loving family life is the greatest legacy you can bestow on your children.

Easy for you to say, Donna! you may be thinking. *But you've never spent a day home alone with my kids!*

True, but I've spent years home alone with my own. In this chapter and the next I want to share with you some practical tips I've gathered for making the most of your time with your children.

a dozen hints for happy children

1. *Eat together.* Gather your family together for mealtimes as much as possible. Make it a positive experience in which family members can talk and share and be accountable to one another. Consider "actually talking to each other" over a plate of food. Hear what went well—or badly—during the day. Enjoy a joke together. Debate an issue. Look forward to a challenge—a report to give at school, an important sales call, a special song to perform at church.[2]

Eating meals together is also an excellent means for teaching table manners to your children. Proper mealtime manners are becoming a lost art in our culture.

When Anissa was growing up, our family ate breakfast and dinner together almost every day. And the family wasn't allowed to eat anything they wanted. They all ate what mom fixed. Dad said, "There will be one meal served at one time. You will demonstrate care for your mother by eating whatever she sets before you. She will not be a slave to you and the kitchen." As Anissa grew older and dinner at home wasn't always possible, we still made sure we sat down together for breakfast.

Family dinner is making a come back. *Child Magazine,* in a 2006 survey, surprised their Food and Nutrition Director Karen Cicero by indicating more than half of the families surveyed gather at the dinner table for a home-cooked meal. In the Fall of 2005, the first Family Pledge Day occurred, drawing more than 1 million families who pledged to have a meal together on September 26, 2005.

The family is the first and often the smallest political unit our children know. The most frequented meeting place for this political unit is the table (change seats one night and see the effect). In biblical times the meal was symbolic of intimate and joyous fellowship. Martin Bubar speaks my heart: "One eats in Holiness and the table becomes an Altar."

In 1996 Dr. Catherine Snow, professor of Harvard Graduate School of Education, revealed after following 65 families over an eight-year period that it was determined that dinnertime was of more value to a child's development than playtime, schooltime, and story time.

Our family continues to make the effort to gather at a table, presented neatly and filled with as much beauty as possible. Our grandchildren pull up their highchairs and add to the merriment. I highly recommend family mealtimes!

2. *Help children not to be bored.* I've never met a child who doesn't occasionally say, "I'm bored." Here are two tips to help you deal with a child's boredom.

First, be creative about filling their days with things to do so they don't have time to be bored. For example, Barbara Johnson tells about a mom who had an ivy-covered hill in her backyard. One day she threw a handful of pennies on the hill, telling her children they could keep the pennies they found. The treasure hunt kept them busy for more than an hour.

Brainstorm a list of boredom-beating ideas for kids with your husband or a friend and keep it handy. When you see your child vegetating in front of the TV you can quickly check your list and say something like, "Let's each take a paper sack and see how much litter we can find in our neighborhood in 30 minutes," or "Let's surprise Daddy by polishing all his shoes," or "Let's play a game of Bible trivia, and the loser serves the lemonade," or "Here's a new Bible storybook I found at the bookstore. Would you like to read it?"

Second, use exercise as an antidote for boredom. No matter how creatively you try to fill their time, your children will still say "I'm bored" at times. Kay, a friend of mine, has a technique for dealing with her three sons when they complain of boredom. For as many years as I can remember, whenever one of her boys said, "I'm bored," Kay would respond, "Great! Give me 50 push-ups, please," or "Run around the block, please," or "Wash the car, please." After using this technique for awhile, Kay discovered that her sons got very good at occupying their time and seldom complained of boredom. The consequences of saying "I'm bored" to their mother taught Kay's boys to be responsible for their own activities.

3. *Get children outdoors.* Let the air, sun, wind movement, natural sounds, rain, and snow, mingle with the unnatural sounds such as horns beeping and sirens running and become part of your children's experiences. My first grandchild was born in Michigan in the late fall. When he was just 10 days old I asked my daughter if I could take him outside to sit. She agreed, and now years later we are still looking for the wind we feel, listening for birds, and wondering where the truck is going. Remember this world was made by God and there are many lessons to see, feel, and learn outdoors. Enlarge the world beyond indoors, TV, computers, and video games by going right outside.

4. *Provide "don't forget to take it to school" boxes.* Do you want to help your kids find everything they need for the day as they're roaring around in the morning trying to get out the door to school? Put a box (or a bag, crate, or basket) at the door of each child's room. If you have more than one child in a room, get one box for each.

Train them to put everything into the box that needs to go to school with them the next day.

For example, when Will finishes his homework at night, his books go into the box. When you fill out the order blank for his school pictures and write the check that must be turned in tomorrow, they go into the box. If tomorrow is gym day, his gym clothes and shoes go into the box. When Will wakes up in the morning, everything he needs to take to school is waiting for him in the box. (By the way, decorating the boxes is another boredom-beating idea you can add to your list.)[3]

5. *Prepare your children to make good decisions.* Good decision-making starts when children are very young. Mothers attending my organizational workshops often say to me, "My child is a pack rat. What should I do?" My first response is, "Your child isn't a pack rat. He just hasn't been taught to make good decisions. He can't decide whether to keep stuff, give it away, or throw it away."

How do you prepare a child to make good decisions? Begin with decision-making in simple, noncritical areas. For example, select three drawings your child has made this week and set them before him. Say, "We don't have enough room in your scrapbook for all three pictures, so let's choose one to keep. Which one shall we keep?"

Initially he may say, "Oh, Mommy, I don't know which one to keep. Which one do you think I should keep?" Don't make the decision for him. Help him talk about the merits of each, but leave the choice to him. It will be difficult for him at first, but soon he will make the decision. Affirm his decision, and discard the other two drawings.

Use this process over and over with your children. As they learn the process on increasingly more important issues, their decision-making skills will be perfected.

6. *Inspect what you expect.* Habits are those behaviors we perform without thinking about them. When I get into the car, I put the key into the ignition, depress the clutch, slip into gear, and drive away

automatically. I operate the car by habit. I brush my teeth at night by habit.

If you want your children to develop good habits, you must inspect what you expect them to do. If you've instructed your children to tidy their rooms, brush their teeth, and hang up their clothes before leaving for school, make sure they have done what you instructed. If you let them off the hook by not checking up on them, you're just making more work for them and yourself. But if you hold them accountable for what they should do, you will help them create good habits of behavior. Once the habits are formed, let your kids go. Make the habits their responsibility to keep.

7. *Don't give your children too many choices.* Don't give them choices too early. In today's world people face a plethora of choices. It is good to have options but it does take training to deal well with choices. I overheard a mother telling a small child perhaps three or four years old, "You may choose your cereal." After she left the aisle I counted the number of choices: 98 different boxes of cereal. Ninety-eight boxes is too many choices for a small child. When allowing your child to make choices, remember to take his personality into consideration. For instance, if he or she tends to be shy, you may have to encourage your child more than a child who is more outgoing.

8. *Help your children make friends.* Michele Borba, author of *Nobody Likes Me, Everybody Hates Me,* offers these tips for jump-starting your children's social life:

- Set a good example yourself. Your little one watches how you interact with people. Model how to strike up a conversation with another parent at the playground. Get together with friends.

- Read all about it. Read some stories to your child that involve making new friends. Discuss the book with them.

- Provide a pickup line. Consider training your child to initiate conversations with other kids using a simple statement or conversation starter. One that works is simply to say, "Hello, my name is…"

- Be where kids are. Children need practice in making friends. Join a playgroup, make regular trips to the park or library for kids' reading times.
- Make plenty of play dates with other kids.
- Work on social skills—theirs, not yours. Explain that good friends share, take turns, listen to each other, and don't bully or hit.
- Encourage your child to explore her interests. Friendships often develop around mutual activities, so help your child get involved with something he or she enjoys.
- Get in sync with your child's friendship style. Some kids are shy and some have no trouble approaching other children.

9. *Give your children confidence in courtesy.* In a society where "me" is first, it's important that you teach your children to be courteous to their elders, including you as their parent. Teach them to open the door for you as you enter a shopping mall or restaurant. Teach them to wait for their elders to be seated before they sit down. Teach them to give up their seat on the bus to someone older or to a mom holding a baby. Teach them to allow their elders to be served first in a buffet line.

If your children's father is in the picture, they should be taught to respect him. Their father is their heritage. A daughter learns of her responsibility to her husband through her dad. A son learns of his responsibility to the family he will have someday through his obedience to his dad. Teaching children to obey their father and you is necessary. If they can't or won't obey you, how will they ever learn to obey God?

Teach them to say "excuse me," "please," and "thank you." If you think your children will learn these courtesies just by growing up, I have news for you—they won't. You have to teach your children common courtesy. It counts for a lifetime!

Some great books on courtesy include *Social Graces* by Ann Platz and Susan Wales. Also check out *A Little Book of Manners for Boys* by Bob and Emilie Barnes and *A Little Book of Manners* (for girls) by Emilie Barnes.

10. *Help your children understand their bodies.* There are an abundance of national fitness programs available for your children. The guidelines vary according to the children's age. The National Association for Sport and Physical Education's 2003 guidelines say:

> Children need to be active and healthy. Sometimes we forget that all that activity and energy they expend is actually essential to their growth and health. One in ten children ages two to five is overweight, according to a release from the President's Council on Physical Fitness and Sports. For children and teens, the number of overweight kids is one in seven! That report says small children need several hours of unstructured movement every day. They should never be inactive for more than 60 minutes. Toddlers need at least 30 minutes of structured activities and preschoolers need at least 60 minutes of structured activities like "follow the leader," "take tiny steps, giant steps," or jump "like a rabbit."

Exercise and food intake go hand in hand. The number of eating disorders are still in epidemic proportions. Pay attention to your children's eating habits after you stop feeding them three meals a day.

11. *Teach Stranger/Danger appropriately.* Sadly, we continue to see an increase of crime. This fact calls parents to teach children how to deal with strangers. The days of sending your children down the block to knock on the door of a "neighbor" without some guidelines are gone.

When Anissa was four years old, my father took her and me out for an Italian dinner. She asked to leave the table to go the restroom. I pointed to the door and sent her on her way. My father responded with, "There could be a dangerous situation facing her." I shrugged his remark off, chalking it up to a doting grandfather, and finished my pasta. Thirty-plus years later parents need to watch every step their children make.

Dr. Robin Goodman of the New York University Child Study Center, as quoted in the Parents Action for Children Organization, gives six tips to help parents and children feel safer when dealing with children:

1. *Parents must have the right attitude and approach:* Parents must set the tone for their children. When parents are calm when discussing tough or scary topics, children will be better able to listen and learn. Parents must monitor their own fear and be careful not to alarm their children.

2. *Consider the child's age.*
   - 3- to 5-year-old children are curious and may be naturally trusting. They also easily respond to attempts by adults to be kind or supportive. Toddlers and preschoolers do not necessarily grasp the long-term consequences of potentially dangerous situations.
   - 6- to 9-year-old school-age children are more capable of understanding right from wrong. They are able to remember information and put it into practice, but may feel overwhelmed in a difficult situation.
   - 10- to 13-year-old children may overestimate their ability to handle a bad situation. They also may feel they should not be scared and be nonchalant in their attitude about risk.

3. *Deliver information in an age-appropriate way.* Younger children will benefit from playing and repeated conversations. Parents of older children can discuss current events or real situations to educate them about danger.
   - *Talk:* Have a discussion with children about safety and strangers. It can be used to find out how a child defines a

"stranger." Parents are often surprised to hear only ugly creatures in storybooks are considered dangerous.

- *Ask:* After talking to children, it is important to ask them what they heard. This allows parents to correct misinformation and determine what needs to be repeated or discussed differently.

- *Show:* It can be helpful for parents to practice with children what they have learned. This can mean going to a mall and having a child ask for help from a clerk or walking through the neighborhood and watching as the child goes to an identified neighbor's house.

- *Know:* Make sure children know who, when, where, and how to get help. For example, they should know their names, address, and phone number; how to dial 911; who will pick them up from school and activities; other friends and families who have been approved.

4. *Monitor media:* Especially when child abductions and murders are in the news, parents should be aware of what their children are watching or hearing. Help them separate fact from fantasy. Parents should be sensitive to any changes in their children's behaviors, especially sleeping problems and nightmares, and seek additional guidance.

12. *Make Memories/Create Traditions.* Close your eyes, Mama, and think of a memory that brings a smile to your face. Was it a party? Holiday? Celebration? Was there a person at the center of the memory? Usually it takes an intentional person to create a memory. Memories are not accidental.

If you have ever overheard a family member say, "We always do it this way," and you scratch your head thinking, "We've done this just once before," you have encountered creating a tradition. Traditions are repeated events that tie a group of people together and make them feel loved or special.

My son-in-law sings "Shaboom, shaboom, yada yada yada" as he shuffles his firstborn off to bed each night. Interestingly, his father sang and shuffled him off each night to "Hi ho, hi ho, it's off to bed we go." This is a generational tradition now. Maybe yours are eating pizza every Saturday, pancakes on Sunday morning made by Dad, attending a parade on Memorial Day, fishing on the first Friday after school is out, or church on Good Friday.

Precious and pleasant memories are a gift. Proverbs 24:3 tells us, "By wisdom a house is built, and by understanding it is established; and by knowledge the rooms are filled with all precious and pleasant riches." Enjoy your children as you create memories and traditions that will last a lifetime.

a few otto mottos

Here are several pithy mottos we used in our home as we raised our child. Mottos are short, pithy, and easy to repeat.

"First and Fast."

We coached our child, "Whatever you don't want to do, do it first and fast." Whether it was completing a school project, getting her books off the kitchen counter, or eating broccoli, we urged her to get it done and get it off her mind.

Distasteful tasks remain distasteful when you keep putting them off. But in the words of Alexander MacLaren, "It is only when they are behind us and done that we begin to find that there is sweetness to be tasted afterwards, and the remembrance of unwelcome duties unhesitatingly done is welcome and pleasant."

"You can do it."

Whenever my child complained, "This is impossible; I can't do it," our immediate response was, "You can do it."

The film *Stand and Deliver* is based on the life of Jaime Escalante, a gifted high school teacher in Los Angeles. Escalante enabled scores of disadvantaged students from the barrio to pass the advanced placement test in mathematics by constantly reminding them, "You can do it."

This is the encouragement your kids need too. Keep reminding them that they can succeed. You can do it, Mom!

"Open a new window."

There's a song in the musical "Mame" in which Mame encourages her nephew to try something new and challenging. "Open a new window," she sings. She doesn't want him to get stuck in a rut. This is a good motto for our kids. Continually challenge them to open new windows, try new things, and look for new opportunities. It's also good advice for moms.

"The common begin, but the uncommon finish."

We used this motto to encourage our child to finish what she started. We wanted her to feel that finishers are unusual and special. Some projects she started could not be completed for reasons beyond her control. But the most common reason for not finishing is lack of perseverance. Challenge your kids to be uncommon by getting the job done.

"Buck up."

This is a motto we used in the middle of a distasteful task when spirits were flagging. Most kids don't like it because it reminds them of a task they would rather weasel out of than complete. Buck up means, "I know it's tough, but it's got to be done. Hang in there."

I even use this motto with mothers of young children. These are hard days. You're tired and weary, and your job as a mom sometimes seems impossible. I know. Just buck up and get it done.

"That's a lie from the pit."

When Anissa was about eight years old, we were sitting at the kitchen table during dinner one night when she said, "I feel fat, dumb, and ugly." Suddenly, before I even realized what I was saying, I waved my finger at her and said in a very severe tone, "That's a lie from the pit of hell. Replace it with the truth." David gasped and Anissa's big brown eyes widened in shock. After a tense moment of silence, we all broke out in laughter at my exaggerated response.

After we composed ourselves, David and I reminded Anissa that she was not fat, dumb, and ugly. It really was a lie she was telling herself, and it had brought discouragement into her life. While this motto is a severe statement, it stuck, and it's used often by all who know us.

Remind your children that God's Word instructs us to tell ourselves the truth. For example, the truth is that we sometimes make mistakes or do dumb things, but we're not dumb. When you catch your children telling lies to themselves, remind them where those lies come from and guide them to the truth.

"Put it back where you got it."

Believe it or not, this is the first complete sentence Anissa uttered. Even though her words were a bit garbled and I was flushed with embarrassment, I was amazed at how early she learned this motto. And she's still following the principle in her adult life.

"Do it at once."

Alexander MacLaren also said, "No unwelcome task becomes any the less unwelcome by putting it off till tomorrow."

Teach your kids not to put off until tomorrow what they can do today.

"Tough Teabags."

Sometimes you need a warm and funny way of saying, "Sorry. What you want can't be done." I was so well known for this saying that some of the teachers at Anissa's school made me a corsage of flowers and teabags to commemorate it.

What are your family mottos? If you think about it, you probably have some. They are the phrases you use in your family to help you accomplish the things in life that are important to you. Talk about them and jot them down the next time you eat together. If you need motto ideas, use some of mine. And if you want more ideas, check out my book *Finding Your Purpose as a Mom*. Remember, your family mottos are likely to be remembered and used by the next generation.

launching your children into the future

Today's lessons are tomorrow's habits.

What's the most important thing to you? No mother has ever responded by telling me "my stove," "my attaché case," or "my work." All of them say "my family," "my husband," or "my children." Isn't this how you would answer?

Of all the tasks of my life, being a wife and mother are the most worthwhile things I have ever done. My relationships with my husband and daughter and her family are the most valuable relationships I have. Nothing has been both as trying and as rewarding as my mothering opportunities. As a mom, you know exactly how I feel.

Think for a moment about what your mothering is accomplishing. Take a look into your children's future. Where are they headed? What will they do? What will they accomplish in life? Will they be a source of encouragement or discouragement to those around them?

What your children become will reflect how you shape them, nurture them, and discipline them today. Are you indulging your children now because it seems easier than confronting them on the tough issues that arise during childhood? Do you realize that an indulged child will likely grow up to be a selfish adult?

When I think of a mom's responsibility to shape her children for the future, I think of the mother of John Newton, the great British evangelist of the late 1700s. Mrs. Newton made a lasting impression on her son. She prayed regularly for him as he grew up, imploring God to keep His hand on the child. She often prayed for him with her hands upon his forehead.

As a young adult, John Newton scorned his mother's faith and set off to see the world. But no matter how far he traveled from his mother, even to the coast of Africa as the captain of a slave ship, he could not escape the remembrance of his mother's prayers. He believed he often felt the softness of his mother's hands on his head.

Years later John Newton acknowledged Christ. He became one of the most influential ministers of the gospel in England. His mother's influence on his life during his childhood was never lost.

How can we launch our children to become responsible, mature, serving adults? Scores of books have been written and theories abound. But lofty child-raising theories often wilt in the heat of the day-to-day experience of actually raising kids. John Wilmot, the earl of Rochester during the seventeenth century, quipped, "Before I got married, I had six theories about children. Now I have six children and no theories." Don't you love it? Experience is the greatest teacher.

I want to share with you several concrete ideas that may help you in your experience of shaping your children and launching them into the future.

set the pace with your example

There are three major qualities our children need to see in our lives: 1) truthfulness in words and actions, 2) faithfulness, and 3) gratitude.

1. *truthfulness*

Are you always truthful with your children? If we tell them lunch in a minute, lunch should be there soon. If we promise we are coming to tie a shoe, we should be there. There should be a ring of truthful authority in our voice that lets them know what we say we mean. Even a small baby responds to a tone of voice that conveys authority. This kind of truthfulness from mother to child builds a very strong foundation for their trust in the truthfulness of our heavenly Father. Proverbs tells us hope deferred makes the heart sad. A yes or no answer is always better than a maybe. Truthfulness has the ring of authenticity.

2. *faithfulness*

Your children need to see faithfulness in your daily life. J.R. Miller says:

> Too many people are not faithful in little things. They are not to be absolutely depended upon. They do not always keep their promises. They break engagements. They do not pay their debts promptly. They come behind time to appointments. They are neglectful and careless in little things. In general they are good people, but their life is honeycombed with small failures.

As we move at record speeds, rushing to and fro, adding more demands to our lives, the need to stress common courtesy is obvious. Being casual can also mean being unreliable. Make your "yes" yes and your "no" no habitually. You will show your children that you can be positively depended upon when you are faithful in the least as well as the greatest tasks in your life. Your life and your character should be consistently true, giving out a light in the world that honors Christ and others.

3. *gratitude*

Your children should see that you look with grateful appreciation and admiration to your Maker for the miracle they are to you. Let your children know you are grateful to God for them.

Make clear to your children that you expect grateful attitudes from them. In the ninth grade, Anissa acted out her lack of gratitude, and I quickly corrected her. I yelled at her, a rare occurrence, and tears came to my eyes as words of disappointment slipped off my tongue and a punishment was issued.

The incident apparently made a lasting impression. During Anissa's junior year in college, she served as a resident assistant in her dorm. I received a phone call from her one evening. "Mom," she said, "I now know what you meant that day you lost your cool about the importance of demonstrating gratefulness." I took a deep breath. She continued, "The women on my floor are grateful for all I do, but they don't show it!" Gratitude takes time to learn.

In addition, another way you set the pace for shaping your children is to get involved in their lives. This means attending their programs and events and taking an active interest in their education. This also takes time.

I was delighted to read Tim Kimmel's newsletter (Kimmel founded Family Matters). In it his wife, Darcy, described her volunteer work in her daughter's school: "I'm helping in my daughter's classroom one afternoon a week and it's such fun. It's like being a little mouse in the corner. In addition to preparing lessons and art projects, helping at activity centers and serving snacks, I also tie a lot of shoes, straighten many barrettes, and give hugs and lots of encouragement."

When Anissa had successfully completed 16 years of formal education, graduating from college in the spring of 1991, she laughingly says, "My mother was my homeroom mother from kindergarten through college." It's quite true. I was a homeroom mother in her schools until she graduated from the eighth grade. During her high school years, I served on the booster club board, and when she entered college, David and I served on a Parents Advisory Council. We stayed involved. I urge you to do the same, whether your children are homeschooled or in private or public school.

making the education choice

In her material entitled "Choosing Your Child's Education," Sherilyn Jameson helps parents make the right choice for each child.

Jameson, who has taught in public and Christian schools as well as homeschooling, wrote, "Each educational choice for your children is a sensitively individual one. The right choice for your children and for your family can be based on conviction, but it cannot become a mandate for all other children, nor for all other families, regardless of how firm your conviction is."

Kay Lybeck, president of the Arizona Education Association, agrees. "No matter how much or how little time parents spend with their children, they are the most important influence in their children's lives—more important than teachers, preachers, peers, or rock stars. This means that parents, whether they know it or not, wield a powerful influence on how their children benefit from school." Our every move is seen and felt by our children. No parent teaches a child to sneeze, smile, laugh, or walk like them, yet children grow up doing all these things like their parents do.

The following list from Jameson's book points out the major pros and cons of public schooling, private Christian schooling, and home-schooling. Although not complete, they will help you evaluate what your education goals are for your children.

Public Schooling

advantages

1. Public school classes can be a mission field—Christians can be "salt and light."
2. Low cost financially.
3. Access to specialized programs such as art, music, physical education/athletics, clubs, computer training, remedial and learning-disabled help, reading advancement, and challenging classes for the "gifted."
4. Children have the opportunity to practice Christian values (with the support of loving, accepting parents).
5. Certified classroom teachers as well as educators with specialized training/certification in their fields: reading specialists, psychologists, speech pathologists, etc.

6. Parental opportunities to have a positive impact on schools, districts, and communities.

disadvantages
1. Large class sizes.
2. Less individualized instruction.
3. Long days, particularly for primary-age children (kindergarten–third grade).
4. Teachers and classmates may not share the same values as your family. Peer pressure can be strong.
5. Poor test scores nationally.
6. Parents have very little direct control over curriculum, teaching methods, etc.

Private Christian Schooling

advantages
1. Educational foundation based on truth—Scripture.
2. Teachers and peers often share the same value system as your family.
3. More positive role models in your child's life.
4. Usually smaller class sizes.
5. Usually a Christian focus. Specifically, the curriculum will reflect the Christian worldview.
6. The school is a coworker with the parents.

disadvantages
1. Enormous financial commitment.
2. Teacher certification may not be required.
3. Specialization can be limited. There can be limitations in course offerings and athletic opportunities.
4. Complacency about Christianity can easily become an issue for your child.

5. Parent passivity and/or involvement can become an issue if they do not maintain the mind-set that their child's successful education is primarily their responsibility.

6. Students can learn to look, speak, and act like a Christian in public but continue to make poor choices in private. They can learn to "talk the talk but not walk the walk."

Homeschooling

advantages

1. Parents instill their own personal/spiritual values into their teaching.

2. Time flexibility and unwasted learning time.

3. Instruction can be individualized; children learn at their own pace and needed corrections can be made immediately.

4. Parental involvement and complete control of a child's education, particularly the curriculum.

5. Peer group essentially mandated by parental choice.

6. Quantity time with family, much less time spent away from home.

disadvantages

1. Major, personal sacrifices of the teaching parent's time, energy, and commitment.

2. Can be very costly financially.

3. Highly sheltered and potentially over-protective environment.

4. Limited access to special programs and facilities unless extra finances are available. Programs such as music, art, foreign languages, and special facilities needed for athletics, science, and drama may not be available.

5. In some states no outside student evaluation is required; it is

often difficult to be objective about your child's progress and abilities.

6. Personal "life" interruptions. It takes an immeasurable amount of organization and self-discipline to do the job of home-teaching well.

Homeschooling restores the home as the center of life and faith for the child and for his parents. The U.S. Census Bureau reports that there were an estimated 1.1 million homeschooled students in the United States in 2003, or roughly 2 percent of the school-age population. A magazine devoted to parenting called homeschooling a "revolution" growing by perhaps as much as 15 to 20 percent per year.

Regardless of your education choices, the home still remains the first school and church every child encounters. Sunday school teachers, educators, tutors, mentors, family members, and childcare workers can help you, but in the end, the child God has given you needs *you* to take authority over his or her life and education.

teach the difference between wants and needs

Kids can do without a lot of things that money can buy if they have love and affirmation. Yet God has given you and your family a specific amount of money each month to steward. You don't need to manufacture poverty in your home to help your children appreciate what they have. But I encourage you to help them understand stewardship and that God owns everything and is the author of everything. He has given them the privilege of stewarding whatever possessions they have.

Teach your children to have a respectful attitude toward their possessions and riches, to hold their hands open, to be willing to offer whatever they have for the use of service. Help them realize that those who are trustworthy with very little can be trusted with much more. Instill in them appreciation and thankfulness for all they have.

always look ahead in your teachings

One day your children will leave home. When they do, will they have learned everything you wanted them to learn? Make a list now of the things you want your children to be knowledgeable about and the areas of responsibility in which you want them to be skilled before they leave. Use this list to guide you. When they finally do leave, they will have learned what you planned for them to learn.

I'm very grateful to my friend June who encouraged me to make such a list when Anissa was very young. Being an overachiever, I listed specific skills I wanted Anissa to master at age 8, 12, 16, and by the time she left home. I wasn't legalistic about it (I tried not to be). If she didn't learn a skill on schedule, it was okay. The list was just a guideline for me.

Anissa went to France as a helper to a missionary family during the summer of her senior year in high school. As she prepared to leave, a friend asked me, "Are you giving her a last-minute crash course so that when she gets there she doesn't make any faux pas?" I realized that I didn't have to give Anissa special instructions. Thanks to my list, I felt comfortable about where she was and what she could handle at her age.

Watch for signs that your children are getting stuck and not growing up emotionally. A close friend tells the story of being born to parents who did not marry until several years after she was born. My friend says that her mother never emotionally grew past those early days of pregnancy and motherhood. At age 55, she was stuck in the same emotional track she was in when she was 15.

The telltale signs of emotional immaturity are an unwillingness to make decisions, accept responsibility, and make commitments. Watch for these signs, and help your kids get past these issues so they can thrive emotionally.

Anissa had an issue that popped up in her life when she was about seven. It was a sticky issue. It needed some mother–daughter time, prayer, talking, teaching, and probably some crying to solve. You know what I did? I buried my head, pretending I didn't see it.

A friend said, "Donna, you need a reality check." She was right. So a few months after the sticky issue popped up I started the process of resolving with Anissa. We talked, cried, and tried to work out the issue so Anissa could make a change and accept what God had planned. It was tiring and painful but necessary. Anything that can be worked out at home in a loving environment with your children will be a blessing to them all the days of their lives. How much easier for Anissa to face the need to forgive at age 9, 11, 13, and 17 than starting to learn this at 33.

One more thought about "letting go." It is easier to let go of things that don't belong to us, so the gentle self-reminders that our children are gifts from God will help. It also helps to watch for the progression of a child's individuation. Anissa loved eggs for the first few years of her life and then one morning, "I don't like eggs." The letting go had begun. She had a mind of her own and was able to choose for herself. This continued as she went to Sunday school and school without me. Next she made friend selections without me, and soon she was gone overnight and then a weeklong camp. Each of her steps showed me about letting go of my girl.

I will never forget the morning she drove my standard transmission car out of our garage by *herself*. She had finished her driving school and passed the state licensing exam. I still recall my thoughts of "can she shift, depress the clutch and gas pedals while she steers the car?" Tears rolled down my face, and I admitted to this huge step of letting go. College and marriage and moving followed.

I know, it is hard and painful. The morning after our girl got engaged I sobbed my heart out knowing she was now Jason's woman and not my little girl. Letting go is not easy but necessary. Prepare now; it does ease the pain.

training vs. teaching

In the early days of your child-rearing, you are going to do much more training than teaching. A two-year-old needs to understand that when you say no, you mean no. While he is unable to understand exactly why you say no, he needs to know how to obey. When he is standing on the edge of the curb and a car is coming down the street, he doesn't understand what that 2,000-pound car will do to his little body if he runs out in front of it. But you do. If you have trained him to stop in his tracks when you say no, he will be safe. When he gets older you can teach him the reasons behind your training.

Training a child through discipline requires that you break his will, not his spirit. When she was 22 months old, Anissa and I took a car trip together to spend a day with a friend. The trip started in fine form, but about 30 minutes into it Anissa reached down to the car radio (these were the days before car seats and having your baby ride in the backseat) and turned it on full blast. I calmly responded, "Anissa, turn the radio down." She refused.

What followed was a 45-minute session by the side of the road between two very strong-willed people. Anissa did not want to turn the radio down. "No," she said. I insisted. I promised to spank. I did spank. "No," she said.

Finally, after many nos, spanks, and tears, Anissa turned the radio down. Then she fell exhausted into the security of my arms, sobbing with relief. I required obedience. The scene has always been a picture to me of what happens when we finally obey the Lord after our will has been in conflict with His. We fall exhausted and sobbing into His arms and are forever changed.

Children need to learn obedience through discipline. Without discipline, the level of obedience in a 16-year-old will be no greater than in a 2-year-old. Do you want your 16-year-old speaking to you and behaving as your 2-year-old does? Of course not. But he will if you don't teach him instant obedience through discipline. As I've heard my dear friend Elisabeth Elliot say many times, "Anything less than instant obedience is disobedience." One caution, however. Be careful not to require more than your child can accomplish at any one time.

Use God's Word to encourage your children to obey. God's Word is a sharp and powerful two-edged sword. It will cut to the marrow of any issue. Teach them and train them early that God's Word is the law, the bottom line for your parenting and discipline. Early on they must know that the Bible is your wellspring of information and direction for raising them.

One of the most important aspects of disciplining children is to look them in the eye and get their attention. The mistake I see most frequently is the mother's failure to get the child's attention when disciplining him.

You see a harried mother in the grocery store with an infant in the cart and a three-year-old racing up and down the aisles touching everything in sight. Whenever the child grabs something, the mother snaps, "Put it back!" When he whines around the gumball machine, she says, "No, you can't have any gum!"

But the child isn't listening, and the mother is beside herself. It's the same thing at home. Mom is directing the child but not interacting with him. She doesn't give the child her attention, and fails to gain his attention, so the misbehavior continues.

Eye contact is by far the most important step in gaining a child's attention for discipline. Sometimes you have to get right in the child's face to obtain good eye contact. When you do, use the child's name: "Johnny, Mama said no!" Repeat it once. If he still fails to obey, then you discipline.

the pass-it-on perspective

As time goes by, you will have opportunities to exercise your mothering gifts and pour out your love on kids other than your own. Your kids will have neighborhood friends, school friends, and church friends, and when they're in your home you have a chance to mentor them. Your own friends have kids that will come under your umbrella of influence. And God will bring other kids into your life just because you're committed to the ministry of motherhood.

Remember, God gave each child the set of parents He planned. Don't try to step into that role. (For help in this important area see my book *Finding a Mentor, Being a Mentor.*)

The other "children of my heart" live in Arizona, Wisconsin,

Texas, California, and Illinois. They belong to me and they don't. They are being parented by some of my nearest and dearest friends, and these dear friends have found me trustworthy enough to allow me to invest time and love in their kids. Others are sent to me via the church I attend, the schools I serve in, and by my neighbors. For instance, there's Thea. I've been to all of Thea's birthday celebrations. I call her friend, and she calls me Auntie Donna with a devotion that touches me deeply.

Amy's mom is one of my closest friends. Amy was my fellow gardener. We dug and planted and watered and harvested together, not only vegetables but a deep relationship as well.

Kim is older. God sent her to us at age 24. At the time she needed a house, and we needed to fill an empty bedroom. We were a perfect match. Kim has been a younger sister, helper, and typist. She is now married and the mother of five!

Jason is my Mexican restaurant buddy. We enjoy conversations over chips, salsa, sarsaparilla, and fried ice cream. He has a pure heart, and I can count on him to tell me the truth.

Christian and Kelly are brothers, two of Craig and Cindy O'Connell's three sons. Christian and Kelly help me bake cookies, tell me riddles, and teach me about G.I. Joe.

Willard, our godchild, helps us keep a focus on our travels. He calls David "Uncle Staush" in a tone of voice that melts my heart.

Sisters Tiffany and Kiendra are daughters of dear friends. We've vacationed, played cards, baked pies, and talked important issues together. Tiffany is now married with three children of her own, but I am still very active in her life and the life of her family. Kiendra is an artist who recently gave her inspiring work to children in an African orphanage. The children loved her art.

The Darocsi daughters, in whose life God honored me with a place, have ministered to me as much as I pray I have ministered to them

And Ted and Jen—friends, pastors, and parents—who are a privilege to watch "do life."

And John is my artist/writer, Ph.D. friend who is now a seminary professor, married, and has two daughters.

A group of 13 young women, whom I call "Lilies," fill my days and hours now as I continue to invest in the next generations.

And of course there's my grandchildren! I love to spend time and energy with them!

My relationships with these young men and women show how at-home moms like you and me can pass on to our children and others what God has given to us. Whatever we're given, we need to pass on. We can invest, pray, drive our children, drive our friends' children, and as women of God be the vehicle to invest in the lives of others.

I am so grateful not only for Anissa, but for all the others God has placed in my life. To me it's the frosting on the cake of being an at-home mom—the ultimate reward!

In his book *Beholding God,* Darien Cooper tells a story of an old monk that reminds me who is really in control as I raise my children.

> "I need oil," said the old monk. So he planted an olive sapling. "Lord," he prayed, "it needs rain that its tender roots may drink and swell. Send gentle showers." The Lord sent gentle showers.
>
> "Lord," prayed the monk, "my tree needs sun. Send sun, I pray Thee." The sun shone, gilding the dripping clouds. "Now frost, my Lord, to brace its tissues," cried the monk. Behold, the little tree stood sparkling with frost, but at evening it died.
>
> Then the monk sought the cell of a brother monk and told his strange experience. "I, too, planted a tree," he said. "See, it thrives well. But I entrust my tree to God. He who made it knows better what it needs than a man like me. I laid no conditions. I fixed not ways or means. 'Lord, send what it needs,' I prayed, 'the storm or sunshine, wind, rain, or frost. Thou hast made it and Thou dost know.'"[1]

It takes more than good intentions to be a good mother. We need the direct intervention of the One who made us and our children. I earnestly trust that these ideas and principles will help you be the best at-home mom you can be. But don't forget to continually pray, "Lord, send what my children need."

9

checking your id

Your education and experiences are
valuable at home.

I met Anita through our church. She shared her insights freely with me on the changes she experienced becoming an at-home mom. Anita married at 22. She had a bachelor of arts degree in education and a determination to teach. Teaching was soon replaced by her own business, corporate offices, employees, and a very nice income. Then, at age 26, Anita became pregnant. She asked herself if she should give up her career to raise her children.

Like many working women I meet, Anita had some critical thoughts about at-home moms. She wondered what they did all day. She also knew some mothers whose homes weren't always neat and tidy and whose children weren't always perfectly groomed and well-behaved. That really troubled her. After all, when she left her office at night everything was put away or straightened, awaiting the next morning's business. She thought women at home were lazy.

Anita had another major concern about being an at-home mom. She just knew if she quit her job to stay at home she would become overweight and dumpy-looking. It was a fear that often over-whelmed her.

Despite her hesitancy and misgivings, Anita felt that she could minister to her family best by staying at home with her new baby. The transition for her was difficult, marked by pressure from her former coworkers to return to the office, fear that she would lose her business sense, and confusion over her identity. But she stood firm and followed through with her commitment.

Anita is now 46 and the mother of three boys, one in college and two still at home. She has been at home for 20 years. She continues making a home and realizes it's okay if it's not always perfect. Her hospitality times are casual. She's been involved in a preschool co-op, carpool, and works part-time via technology. She's also created some art masterpieces. "It's working," she says, "and I'm not overweight or dumpy-looking." Anita is doing a fine job of raising her sons and modeling godly traits.

solving your identity crisis

If you were influenced by the women's movement in the 1990s, you may think a lot like Anita used to. The message you received from society about your identity was loud and clear: You are what you do. The world's priorities, which center on success, motivation, production, personal worth, and so on, affected your self-perception. And while the stay-at-home movement is gaining momentum, our culture still strongly reinforces the idea that your identity as a woman is primarily derived from your job or career or the abundance of volunteer work you do.

Consequently, when you transition from work to home, you may experience an identity crisis. "Who am I?" you ask. "My job title, my image, my seniority, my education, my skills, my salary, my perks— they all went out the window when I quit my job. I'm just a wife and mother. I've lost my identity."

Rest assured: You did not lose your identity when the laundry room replaced the board room as your center of operations. Your identity is not confined to your job—it never was! Your true identity is in Christ.

You are a child of God, gifted and equipped to serve Him. You haven't lost your identity; you've simply moved it! Your gifts and abilities have been relocated to a new arena—you have shifted your priorities.

Everything about your life may look different to you, but you are still the same. You brought all your skills, education, experiences, personality style, and spiritual gifts with you to be used in your new environment. Your ability to problem-solve at work can be employed at home. The energy you expended at work can now be channeled to the home front. Your vibrant personality will now primarily benefit your family instead of your employer, coworkers, and clients. That's pretty exciting!

Your mothering will be an expression of who you are just as your job was. Every morsel of your education and life experience can be utilized in child-rearing, from your master's degree in art history to your volunteer work with the cancer walks. All your competencies and knowledge are now available as a base for your unique expression of mothering. You have the great opportunity to adapt what you know and what you have experienced to your new full-time environment.

In my opinion, the greatest problem women face today relates to their sense of identity. It's not fear of failure or the hurtful events of the past. The greatest problem among women today is unhealthy comparisons.

the comparison trap

You've heard yourself say or think, "If I had her figure, her husband, her home, her well-behaved children, and her nurturing parents, I'd be _____" (fill in the blank). Comparisons like these start early. I overheard a third-grade girl complain, "If I had her iPod, the girls would like me too." We compare ourselves to other women every day of our lives.

Comparisons like these are a form of discontentment. Yet you have no reason to be discontent. The God of the universe created you individually and equipped you for your good and His glory. What a personal affront it is to Him to complain about how He made you by saying, "If only I had..."

On an airplane returning from Utah I chatted with a woman who was around 35 years old. She had a full-time job, a husband, three children, a nice home, and loving parents, each of whom needed her time and attention. Needless to say, her plate was full.

When I asked why she worked (a favorite question of mine), tears burst from her eyes as she responded, "I kept hearing from friends, reading in the newspaper, and seeing on TV the astronomical numbers of women who have gone back to work. I thought, *If they can do it so can I.* Now I know I can't. I'm worn out all the time, my children are growing up without me, I never see my friends, and recently I've started seeing signs of stress in my marriage."

This dear woman is the classic illustration of the results of unhealthy comparisons. She compared herself to society's depiction of the modern woman. She compared herself to a statistic, and it was ruining her life. Later she contacted me, and I was glad to hear that she had made some radical changes in her life. She was beginning her journey back home.

sorting through the voices

Through the years I have mentored and counseled many young women (read my book *Finding a Mentor, Being a Mentor*), and in recent years I have noted an increased number of influences in their lives, including: books, TV, periodicals, newspapers, the Bible, websites, blog sites, conferences, and seminars. There are also an increased number of relationships due to technology, older women, relatives, and openness to professional counseling. Getting the "voices" into your world is not as difficult as sorting which voice to pay attention to and when. This requires wisdom.

Where do you find the direction you need for being yourself as an at-home mom amid all the criticism from the outside world and the temptation to make unhealthy comparisons coming from within?

You need a director—someone who knows you and can help you understand how your unique gifts and abilities can be applied at home. That director is Jesus.

Identifying Himself as the good shepherd, Jesus said, "The sheep hear his voice, and he calls his own sheep by name, and leads them out...He goes before them, and the sheep follow him because they know his voice" (John 10:3-4). The director of your life is the shepherd of your soul, Jesus Christ. He is committed to nourishing you and helping you when you feel lost. All you have to do is listen for His voice and follow Him.

The problem is the many voices vying for your attention and trying to direct your life as a mother. They are all around you:

> "Anyone can mother your children. You don't need to be there all the time."

> "These are the best earning days of your life. You can have it all and have it now. Don't let your kids keep you from financial success."

> "You need to be a good steward of the expensive education you received. Staying at home is a waste of good money."

> "Your children are a gift from God. He will make sure they are raised right when you're not at home."

You must choose which voice you will listen to and heed. You must decide who will be the director of your life as a mother: the Lord or others around you. The voice you heed is the director you've chosen. Choose carefully.

Sometimes these other voices are from well-meaning loved ones and friends. Pam came up to talk to me after I finished speaking. She waited as I chatted with a number of ladies, signed a few books, and listened to a few stories.

"I'm a lawyer and I have a problem," she began. "Can you help me?"

"I'll try," I said. Pam went on:

> I was raised by uneducated parents who immigrated from Poland. They paid for my education at great personal sacrifice. I

finished law school at 26 and joined a fine law firm in New York. Then I married at 29, and now at 32 I'm ready to start a family.

My parents are elated about being grandparents. But they're furious that I want to be a stay-at-home mom. They accuse me of not being grateful for what they did to secure my education.

Pam loved and respected her parents. She wanted to show honor for them. But their angry demands on her life were voices of confusion. You may have the same experience with your parents, other relatives, or friends. You must decide to be a follower of Jesus and let Him be the director of your life, then you need to subjugate all other influences to His Lordship. As you become accustomed to His voice, discerning other voices will become easier, and you will find freedom and security in doing what you know is right for you.

As you listen to the Shepherd's voice, be aware that His directions won't always sound logical. Leaving a good job and helpful second income to transition into full-time motherhood doesn't sound logical, and you may not see any immediate evidence that it will work out. But if the director of your life is calling you to do it, be confident that He will make a way for it to happen. Say often, "Speak, Lord. Your servant is listening."

For example, let me draw your attention to the story of the children of Israel as they stood at the edge of the Red Sea after leaving Egypt. Picture the setting. The Red Sea lay before them, mountains rose on either side of them, and the Egyptian army was charging up behind them. They were trapped, and they began to panic. If there was ever a time for action, this was it.

But Moses relayed a thoroughly illogical command from the Lord: "Do not be afraid. Stand still, and see the salvation of the Lord" (Exodus 14:13 NKJV). The most natural feeling in that situation would be fear. God told them not to be afraid. The most natural response would be to turn and fight, run into the hills for cover, or start swimming. God told them to stand still. It didn't sound logical, but as they obeyed the sea parted and they were saved.

God is a trustworthy director. He knows what He's doing. He

says, "I know the plans that I have for you...plans for welfare and not for calamity to give you a future and a hope" (Jeremiah 29:11). He has called you to be an at-home mom, and He will make a way for it to happen. Listen to His voice, and don't be afraid.

It takes courage to leave work and be an at-home mom. Be strong, stand still, and listen to the voice of the God who created you and may be calling you to stay at home. Do what you can do. Don't compare yourself to anyone. Don't worry about your identity now that you are an at-home mom. You are a child of God, and He can use everything you are to minister to Him and to your family. Rest in your identity in Christ. The fear of failing in your new role will vanish as you trust Him and rest in Him.

In her book *Travel Tips from a Reluctant Traveler,* actress and author Jeanette Clift George tells a charming story that has become one of my favorites. I share it with moms across America to encourage them to be themselves.

Jeanette was speaking at a luncheon for 400 ladies in the civic auditorium of a city in Oklahoma. As she picked up her fork to begin eating, she noticed that two rose-petaled radishes adorned her salad. She was impressed that someone took the time to pretty up two radishes just for her.

Then she noticed that each salad in the building had two neatly curled radishes. She turned to the lady sitting beside her and remarked how impressed she was with the nearly 800 hand-decorated radishes. "Marietta does those," Jeanette was told. "She says that's her contribution."

After lunch Jeanette was asked if she would like to meet Marietta, and she said yes. She was ushered into the kitchen and introduced to the gray-haired "lady-of-the-radishes," who was wearing a pink-print apron over a dark-green cotton dress. Jeanette greeted Marietta and expressed her appreciation for the festive-looking radishes. Then she returned to the luncheon for the program.

Jeanette spoke, and there was an encouraging response from the ladies. At the close of the program, the hostess ushered Jeanette to a waiting car in a heavy rainstorm. A lady with a large polka-dot umbrella that had collapsed on one side was waiting beside the car. It was Marietta.

Jeanette slipped inside the car, and Marietta crouched down close to the window. "Just remember," she said to Jeanette, "you keep telling people about Jesus, and I'll keep curling radishes."

Jeanette concludes the story, "The rain and my tears splattered the picture of her face as we started the car and backed out of the driveway. Nothing of that moment has faded in my memory. She and I waved to each other as long as we were joined in view. And, dear Marietta, I haven't forgotten. We are to do our two jobs in the love of Him who does all things well."[1]

It doesn't matter if you are a lady who makes speeches, a lady who curls radishes, or a lady at home who makes peanut butter-and-jelly sandwiches. We are who we are by God's grace, and we do what we do in response to His loving voice.

what is a mom worth?

"People might think that stay-at-home moms are sitting around eating Bon-Bons and watching soaps, when in reality we're working several jobs at once. And we're doing it 24/7 with no vacation days, holidays, or even sick days," said Jen Singer, creator of www.momma said.net, a Forbes Best of the Web site for at-home mothers. Singer added, "Many stay-at-home moms are on the job upwards of 100 hours a week. That would be a whole lot of overtime if we got paid."

Stay-at-home mothers wear many hats. They're the family CEO, the daycare provider, accountant, chauffeur, counselor, chef, nurse, laundress, entertainer, personal stylist, and educator. Based on a 100-hour work week, Salary.com has estimated that a fair wage for the typical at-home mom would be $134,121 per year for executing all of her daily tasks.

"Mothers are responsible for the mental and physical well-being of the family—putting a price on that isn't easy," said Lena Bottos, compensation market analyst for Salary.com. "But we looked at it as what you would have to pay other people to do the same work if the mom weren't there."

Even if these mothers were getting paid what they'd be worth on the market, Bottos added that they still wouldn't be adequately compensated. "When you take into account that it represents a 100-hour work week, and doesn't even begin to factor in that they are on call 24 hours a day, it's not so large. Plus, stay-at-home moms get no benefits in terms of pension or 401(k)."

Salary.com provides these 2005 stats for at-home moms:

Daycare center/teacher (15.7 hours)	$ 10,817
Van driver (4.2)	3,334
Housekeeper (22.1)	10,980
Cook (13.6)	10,862
CEO (4.2)	35,971
Laundry machine operator (6.7)	3,133
Janitor (6.3)	3,713
Psychologist (3.9)	7,176
Facilities Manager (5.8)	11,508
Computer Operator (9.1)	7,151
Base pay (40)	45,697
Overtime (51.6)	88,424
Mom's salary (91.6)	**$134,121**

Your worth in dollars and cents is very impressive, you will agree. Let me remind you that your real worth is in how God made you and the investment you are making in your home.

Every experience and level of education that you have is being used in the lives of your family, daily. I applaud you.

creating a dot.calm world

One thing women have going for them is technology. Just look around you at the technological toys and trinkets you use and take for granted. Are you an e-mail maven? Can you move across the internet with ease? Do you research your child's health symptoms on the internet before you call the doctor? Is Google more than a funny word? How about your iPod? Is a cell phone on your hip more often than a two-year-old? Are your phone, TV, and camera digital? Is a chip to you something more than a fattening snack? Not to mention all the technology servants in your home, like your appliances and cooking and cleaning devices. Maybe your coffee comes from a contraption that was unknown ten years ago. Take a look around your home. Technology is everywhere.

It's a dot.com world. Technology adds a lot to our ability to connect and gather information. Mostly it's a good thing—tools useful to help us cope with a complex and busy life. But dot.com is not calm. Technology is also intrusive...or can be if you are not careful. An article in *Forbes* magazine put it succinctly: "24/7 has become the most terrifying phrase in modern life." How do you create a dot.*calm* environment for yourself and your family in the midst of a dot.com world? That's the challenge.

creating a calm home

I remember the day when I thought the only answer to the stress of busyness at home was to make a huge banner and wrap it around the outside of my house. The banner reads:

DO NOT DISTURB!

That's one way to create a calm home—shut everyone and everything out. But that only keeps the outside, outside. It doesn't deal with the commotion within. Calm begins within; calm begins with you.

Anxiety is the enemy of calm. What brings anxiety into your home and into your heart? It's different for each woman. In my case I grew up in a chaotic home where nothing was predictable, shouting and arguing was normal, and everyone seemed angry. If you grew up as I did, you can smell chaos a mile away. I become anxious in the midst of chaos. Calm for me looks a lot like an orderly home where words are soft and things happen in some sort of order. It's a place where people are acting, not reacting. Proverbs says a gentle answer turns away wrath. Soft words are part of my effort to create a calm home.

Busyness also is a cause of anxiety and stress. Busyness and calm do not easily coexist. It's kind of like light and dark, the one eliminates the other. But busyness is not something new to our culture. Douglas T. Miller, in *Then Was the Future: The North in the Age of Jackson 1815–1850,* quotes a man who settled in the United States in the 1820s:

> The Americans seem to know no greater pleasure than that of going on fast, and accomplishing large distances in comparatively short times...This continual motion of the Americans...resembles, on a huge scale, the vibrations of a pendulum...This state of incessant excitement gives to the American an air of busy inquietude...which, in fact constitutes their principal happiness.

Today's technology only makes busyness more epidemic. Do you think we have made much progress in the battle against busyness? I think we embrace busyness and make it a virtue when it can fairly be seen as a vice. And it definitely acts as a negative where calm is concerned.

Much has been written about busyness. The Soccer Mom Syndrome is a title given to busy mothers hustling kids from one event to the other. A home characterized by calm has to confront the burden of busyness. It begins with you. If your heart is calm, you can move toward creating a calm home. You set the temperature of your home in terms of commotion and stress. If you are at peace, the temperature is lowered significantly.

creating a calm heart

A sense of calm is more than keeping yourself under control. If you are full of internal turmoil, eventually it will leak out. You will lose patience. You may use avoidance to deal with your unquiet spirit. Unfortunately your stress will eventually rise to the surface with even greater force. Remember, calm comes from the heart. Do you need heart surgery?

The first step is to examine your heart. Are you really at peace or are you tense? What are you feeling? What are your thoughts centered on? Ask God to reveal the sources of your sense of unrest and anxiety.

Next you need to deal with what you find. So you are anxious about money. Or maybe the source of your unsettled spirit is that others seem to have more than you do. Maybe it's an underlying fear of some kind, a fear that you're not the best mother you can be or that you feel responsible for everything that goes wrong in your home. Maybe you have regrets about your past or worries about your future. I don't know what your particular fears are, but everyone has them to some degree.

Yes, every woman has wounds or fears that eat away at her peaceful heart. Some of them are real and some are imagined; regardless, they drain the joy that might otherwise fill your heart. And fatigue magnifies whatever is creating an unsettled heart. As a mom, I know you experience fatigue.

How do you deal with worry? The psalmist tells us to ask God to search our hearts, to know our hearts and see if there is any hurtful way in us (Psalm 139:23-24). He will illuminate the inside if we just ask Him.

Once we identify the disquieting conditions, we can deal with them. Even a broken heart can be mended. So the first thing we need to do is turn to God and rest in His promises to us. The following are a great place to begin.

> I waited patiently for the Lord; and He inclined to me, and heard my cry. He brought me up out of the pit of destruction, out of the miry clay; and He set my feet upon a rock making my footsteps firm. And He put a new song in my mouth, a song of praise to our God (Psalm 40:1-3).

> Even though I walk through the valley of the shadow of death, I fear no evil; for Thou art with me (Psalm 23:4).

> Hear my cry, O God; give heed to my prayer. From the end of the earth I call to Thee, when my heart is faint; Lead me to the rock that is higher than I (Psalm 61:1-2).

> Cast your burden upon the LORD, and He will sustain you; He will never allow the righteous to be shaken (Psalm 55:22).

> Be anxious for nothing, but in everything by prayer and supplication with thanksgiving let your requests be made known to God. And the peace of God, which surpasses all comprehension shall guard your hearts and your minds in Christ Jesus (Philippians 4:6).

Unload your burdens. Make prayer for a calm heart part of your daily meditation. Watch for the peace that passes all understanding.

While reading a biography on the life of Martin Luther, I found a nugget that proved to be pure gold in my personal life. The nugget stated that Luther had "leisure time with God." These four words ruminated within me for some months and caused me to try some leisure time with God. I set an appointment with myself and God. I prepared by selecting a place and making a plan. What followed was two hours in my prettiest room with a few inspiring books, my yellow pad, a pen, my Bible, and listening ears.

This new way of meeting with God began a process that continues today. I found making a plan that called for no agenda allowed me to meet with God and be comfortable, be casual, be willing to let whatever came to my mind or whatever I read bring me growth, calm, assurance, and yes, even correction. Over the years, the leisure time grew from two hours to four hours to six hours and then to a full day each week. "Wait a minute!" you're saying. "I am a mother of small children." You may not be able to dedicate an entire day to meditation with God, but make sure you set aside some time for Him. If you have an opportunity for childcare of any sort—babysitting co-op, trade time, grandparents, finances to hire a sitter—consider using that for a leisure time with God. It will be life-changing, I promise!

What else can you do to cultivate calm in your home and in your heart?

slow down

An Associated Press poll some time ago called us an impatient nation. From the Department of Motor Vehicles to the grocery store, we're in a hurry. Trevor Tompson, an AP manager, analyzes the poll as follows:

- People lose patience in line after 17 minutes, the phone in 9 minutes
- Women are more patient then men
- People with higher levels of income and education demonstrate impatience quicker that those with less education and income
- Urban folks are a little less patient about waiting in a store or office than people in the suburbs[1]

Hurry concepts are foreign to children until we teach them. Make every effort to give your children opportunities to work at their own pace. And consider a slower pace for yourself.

rest

Rest is critical to our emotional, mental, and physical health. The shocking news of a college senior who took his life a few weeks prior to graduation stunned Westmont College president Stan Gaede. His wife Judy responded, "I think he was looking for some rest. All his life he seemed to be in pursuit of perfection. Socially, academically, athletically, he seemed to be on a quest for success. Indeed, from the outside, it appears he found it. Only it wasn't enough. The one thing he couldn't find was rest. Rest from the chase; rest from the endless pursuit."

You will find calm when you define success with God's terms and choose to resist today's culture that screams, "More, more!"

Along with the importance of rest is the strength we can draw from solitude and communion with God.

silence

There is a natural rhythm not only of work and rest, but of sound and silence through the beginning and ending of each day. Monks have long understood the delight in silence, and the trend is catching on. Approximately half of Amtrak's trains now boast a quiet car. Ed Moose, owner of S.F. Eatery, is quoted as having said, "Silence is a lot more than the absence of noise, but getting rid of noise is a good beginning." Look around your home and see what causes noise: TV, radio, iPods, computers, CD players, telephones, fax machines, toys with batteries, most machines, lawn mowers, blenders. Turn them off.

Establish a quiet time for yourself and your children. It might take some time to get used to, but once you have created a habit of having a time of silence, you'll wonder how you lived without this break.

God wants to guide and direct us. He has much to say to us. It is His desire that we stop and quiet our souls, inviting and respecting His presence into our lives. Develop listening ears for God. He will calm your heart and spirit. And we can't talk about communion with

God without emphasizing the importance of His Word. Get into the Bible. Talk to your children about the importance of studying Scripture and help them apply what they learn to their lives. Show them how you draw strength, wisdom, and peace from the Bible.

consider morning pages

Morning pages are a discipline that wakes up your mind, settles your spirit, allows your creativity to flow, and acts as a censor to your thoughts and concerns. Simply put your pen on the paper and write for three pages. *Yes, even if you only write "I have nothing to say"!* I assure you—your heart will spill and the pen will run as you declutter your spirit and calmness comes.

continuous communion

The ability to keep God in my every thought and action is my deep desire, but the noises and activities of my world work against me. The following men inspired me to center my life in "paying attention" to God. Brother Lawrence, the monk who wrote *Practicing the Presence of God,* suggested we need to "practice" being in God's presence in every moment, in every activity. Jean-Pierre De Caussade described the present moment as a "Sacrament." Frank Laubach described his various experiments at communing with God as "constant communion."

One year of my life, I wore a watch that chimed every hour on the hour. (Yes, I drove my friends and family crazy.) Every hour on the hour I paused for 15 seconds and looked attentively at God's creation before me. I told no one of my experiment. The experience was life altering. Try it! Or create your own experiment to help you keep in continual contact with God.

choose cheerfulness

Cheerfulness is a choice! If you have never consider this fact, please do. The circumstances of our lives are in constant change and flux. As the world speeds up and becomes more complicated, we have a choice in our response. The book of Proverbs describes a joyful heart (a merry heart) as good medicine. Cheerfulness is contagious and can diffuse others from a sour disposition. Consider cheerfulness daily.

treasure the bible

I love to ask questions. Finding out how things work, why something is being done, and information that will help me live my life is very important. I have never asked a question that I could not find the answer in the Bible, including:

How shall I spend my time?
Whom shall I marry?
How shall I parent?
What should I do when someone hurts me?
What is the definition of a friend?

The Bible is a treasure designed to answer our questions and the questions children ask. Know the Bible!

thoughts from the mount of blessing

Let me close this chapter with a profound quote by an unknown, but very insightful author:

If you have given yourself to God, to do His work, you have no need to be anxious for tomorrow. When we take into our hands the management of things with which we have to do, and depend on our own wisdom for success, we are taking on a burden God has not given us and are trying to bear it without His aid. We are taking upon ourselves the responsibility that belongs to God, and thus are really putting ourselves in His place. We may well have anxiety and anticipate danger and loss, for it is certain to befall us. But when we really believe that God loves us and means to do us good, we shall cease to worry about the future. We shall trust God as a child trusts a loving parent. Then our troubles and torments will disappear, for our will is swallowed up in the will of God.

finding time for growth

Did you hear about the census-taker who noted, "No occupation, just a stay-at-home mom"? I've heard he's still in traction!

All jokes aside, every at-home mom will identify with the harried woman depicted in this humorous but uncomfortably realistic poem by Marshall H. Hart:

What Do Women Do All Day?

Every minute, to and fro,
That's the way my hours go;
Bring me this, and take me that,
Feed the dog, and take out the cat.

Standing up, I eat my toast,
Drink my coffee, thaw the roast.
Empty the garbage, make the bed,
Rush to church, then wash my head.

Sweep the kitchen, wax the floor,
Scrub the woodwork, clean the doors;
Scour the bathtub, then myself;
Vacuum carpets, straighten shelves.

Eat my sandwich on the run ...
Now my afternoon's begun.
To the baseball game I go,
When will there be time to sew?

Meet the teacher, stop the fight,
See the dentist, fly the kite.
Help with homework, do the wash,
Iron the clothes, put on the squash.

Shop for groceries, cash a check,
Fight the crowds, now I'm a wreck;
Dinner time it soon will be,
"What's for dinner?" they ask.
Wait and see.

Dirty dishes crowd the sink,
Next there's popcorn, then a drink.
Will they never go to bed?
Will I ever get ahead?

"Bring me water." "Get the light."
Turn off the TV, lock the bike.
"Where's my pillow?" "Hear my prayers."
"Did you lock the door downstairs?"

At last in bed, my spouse and I,
Too tired to move, too weak to cry.
But e'er I doze, I hear him say,
"What do women do all day?"[1]

Time for yourself, for God, and for growth? You may have a baby on each hip and think you have no time for anything but keeping them clean, dry, fed, and safe. But at-home moms just like you are learning how to carve some minutes into the day for personal development. The key is a little planning and preparation and the determination to find a place for your personal life.

time for spiritual nurture

Susannah Wesley, the mother of John, Charles, and 15 others, devoted one hour each day to prayer. And she didn't have a microwave, washing machine, or dishwasher! She allowed nothing to interrupt her personal time with God. Often her children tried and failed. When visitors came during Susannah's hour of prayer, the children awkwardly explained that their mother was unavailable. I marvel at the discipline and accomplishment of this devoted Christian mother! What a legacy for her sons and daughters.

How did she ever find the time? Impossible as it may seem, there is always time in your day to do the things your heart desires and God wills. Every day holds minutes or hours for prayer, Bible study, and reflection if you make them a priority. The key is working to make it happen. We tend to make the time to do what we want to do.

We are always seeking to make ourselves more attractive for the ones we love. No matter how busy we are, somehow we find time to properly dress and groom ourselves for the occasions of the day. Leon Eloy, a Renaissance writer, said, "The holier a woman is, the more attractive she is as a woman." Think of your efforts at developing your spiritual life as an investment in making yourself a more attractive woman.

I can almost hear you saying, "Get real, Donna. I hardly have enough time in my day to get through all the normal crises, let alone have time for Bible study, prayer, and other activities. Maintaining consistent spiritual nurture seems impossible. How can I do it?"

Let me answer your question with another question: How do you eat an elephant? (No, I'm not crazy. I'm making a point.) Answer: One bite at a time. The list of things we must do and want to do each day is like an elephant—huge and intimidating. You can't swallow it all at once, but you can handle it a bite at a time.

For example, I put off painting my dining room for three years because I just couldn't take two or three days off from life to do the job. I realized I was trying to swallow the elephant whole. I decided to break the project into weekly jobs of one to two hours each and spread it out over a few weeks so I could get it done.

The first week I shopped for the paint. The second week I moved the furniture from one wall into the family room. In successive weeks I washed the walls one at a time, taped the woodwork, rolled on the paint, finished the trim, cleaned the carpet, and moved back in. Yes, I had to live with a mess for a few weeks. The process wasn't my first choice, but in two-and-a-half weeks I got the job done.

Look at your personal devotional life the same way. As much as you might want to and need to, you may not have a whole day to devote to Bible study and prayer. But if you approach your spiritual nurture one bite at a time, you can accomplish a lot.

Take Bible study, for instance. When I was 16, I invited the God of the universe to be the Lord of my life. Soon I wanted to get involved in personal Bible study. But for the next 10 years of my life I studied the Bible very little because I wasn't sure how to go about it. I felt that I had to sit down for a couple of hours a day and labor over the Scriptures like a theologian. I couldn't find the time or the stamina for that. I learned 10 hard years later that productive Bible study can be accomplished even in a few minutes.

Here's an idea. Prayerfully select the passages or topics you want to study. Or consider reading one book of the New Testament over and over again daily as your devotional reading until you become familiar with it. Commit at least five to eight minutes a day to being in God's Word. Try to schedule it for the same time every day. Get up early if you must.

When you sit down with your Bible, divide your allotted time in half. Devote the first half to inductive Bible study, gathering the meaning of the content, context, and language. What is God teaching you in this passage? Use the second half of your time for devotional response, worshiping and praising God for what He has done in your life and asking God to apply the passage to your life.

Here's another idea. If your children are small and must be watched constantly, keep a Bible in every room of the house. For example, when your child is bathing, you can pull the Bible from under the sink, sit beside the tub, and read a few verses. When he's playing in the family room, you can read from a Bible you keep on a nearby bookshelf. You can grab several minutes for Bible study as you follow your child around the house.

Another way to enrich your devotional life is to keep a journal or a diary. A written journal is a wonderful chronicle of your hopes and prayers and God's daily provision for you and your family. Malachi 3:16 states: "Then those who feared the LORD spoke to one another, and the LORD gave attention and heard it, and a book of remembrance was written before Him for those who fear the LORD and who esteem His name." Perhaps your spiritual life could be enriched by keeping a written book of remembrances.

My journal is a simple three-ring notebook with lined paper, the same kind of notebook you used in school. I always carry paper with me. I make notes of happenings and write little prayers throughout the day. For example, sometimes when I'm watching TV a word is spoken or a song is sung that brings great conviction or encouragement to my heart. I bring out my paper and jot a paragraph about it.

You can create a computerized journal on your laptop. Even though I love the act of writing, there are times when my head and heart are so full that I pound out my thoughts on the keyboard.

When will you have time to write in your journal? Again, grab any available moments. I often write when I'm waiting at the doctor's or dentist's office. At the end of the day I insert my written pages into my notebook.

The following article by Eileen Pollinger has encouraged me to pursue personal spiritual nurture using all the means at my disposal. Perhaps it will help you too.

> I was walking by Seattle's Lake Union with a friend when she exclaimed, "Look at the deep diving ducks!" In the water bobbed several black-and-white ducks. My friend, a former parks service naturalist, explained that they don't just dip their heads in the water to feed, they dive to the bottom where food supplies are richer.

Most ducks are capable of deep diving, but are content to feed on the surface!

How often we Christians feed on the surface! We munch on good sermons, gulp good books by Christian leaders, take a nip of Christian radio, nibble on taped messages, snack on devotions. We are content with these when a feast of gourmet food and clear, thirst-quenching water awaits us as we dive into the Scriptures seeking to know God better, to learn God's likes and dislikes, God's plans, God's thoughts, God's vision. The surface food is necessary and nourishing, but the best is discovered when we dive deeply and spend time studying God's Word, learning what the Holy Spirit wants to teach us.[2]

Are you a deep-diving duck? Are you a mother who is digging deeply to find what God has called you to be as a person and as a parent?

time for personal growth

You will only build and improve your character as a person by giving careful attention to your personal growth. Kay Arthur, founder of Precepts Ministries, told me once, "What you do will be worth only as much as who you are." Who are you? What are you becoming? Do you give as much attention to your personal growth as you do to your children's personal growth?

How can at-home moms ensure purposeful emotional and intellectual growth, especially with a house full of kids? As freelance writer and stay-at-home mom Jan Johnson suggests, "Full-time motherhood requires the creativity of Thomas Edison, the diplomacy of Henry Kissinger, and the patience of Mother Teresa. Some days you get lost in the job description."[3] Here are some suggestions to get you started.

Allow time for reading books that stretch your mind. Do what Brother Lawrence recommends in *Practicing the Presence of God:* "Fill and nourish your soul with high notions of God, which yield you great joy in being devoted to Him. I call it continuous communion."

As with other areas of personal development, you'll have to fit your reading in where and when you can. When our daughter, Anissa, was small, I always kept a major book, something I was really interested in reading, in the bathroom. Every time I visited the bathroom I would read a paragraph or two and mull it over. You'll be amazed how much soul nourishment you can gain by reading a paragraph during a spare moment. For example, you can read the published journals of Francis Schaeffer or Jim Elliot one entry at a time. A friend reads more than six books annually by reading 15 minutes before bedtime.

Another means for encouraging personal growth is committing yourself to an accountability group. In 1985, a sister in Christ and I decided we needed to be part of a small group of women who were willing to commit themselves to each other for personal and individual growth for life. We sought out women who were spiritually like-minded. Six of us gathered together and founded what we lovingly call our Chaber Group. ("Chaber" is Hebrew, meaning "bound together." We still don't know if we pronounce it properly!)

My Chaber Group is committed to authenticity and mutual love for one another. We meet regularly. Our focus is sharing who we are and how we are affected by our various circumstances. The emphasis is always on what God is teaching us in these situations. Our little group has inspired great personal growth in my life.

No matter what your group's goal or length of commitment is, meeting with a small group of women will change your life. I have even heard husbands say, "I help her get to her group. She's better because of those ladies."

Setting and meeting worthy goals also produces personal growth. Goals are often confused with desires. A desire is something you want to do that requires someone else's cooperation for accomplishment. But a goal is something you can accomplish that cannot be hindered by someone else. Other people can block your desires, but only you can block your goals. Working to fulfill desires often leads to disappointment. But working to fulfill goals leads to growth.

For example, many women make it their goal to have a good

marriage. No wonder they become disillusioned when their husbands fail to live up to their expectations. Having a good marriage is a wonderful desire, but it's not a realistic goal because it requires your husband's cooperation. No matter what kind of wife you choose to be, if your husband is uncooperative, your goal is blocked.

What is a good goal for your marriage? To be a loving, supportive wife. It's something you can accomplish no matter what your husband does. And as you work on this goal you will be doing your part toward fulfilling your desire for a good marriage.

Consider another example. Suppose you have a friend who is in debt. Should you make it your goal to get her out of debt? That may be a good desire, but it's not a good goal because your friend must cooperate for it to be accomplished. Rather, you can make it your goal to support her and encourage her if she makes it her goal to change her financial status. Even if she never saves a dime, you can grow as a supportive, encouraging friend.

What about your desires and goals? Have you separated them in your thinking, or are they all mixed together? Perhaps this is why you have so much trouble accomplishing your "goals." They are really desires that your husband, your children, or others have blocked. I encourage you to separate your desires from your goals, and focus on fulfilling those things you have control over. As you do, I assure you that you will experience greater success in personal growth.

In her article, "Survival Strategies for Stay-at-Home Moms," Jan Johnson offers seven excellent ideas to help you establish some priorities for personal growth.

1. *Set aside time for yourself.* One mom maneuvers her two children into the same nap schedule to secure one to two uninterrupted hours for devotions, resting, letter-writing, etc. Another arranges a weekly three-hour play session for her daughter with an older lady from her church. Others rely on babysitting co-ops or neighborhood teenagers for needed breaks in the routine.

2. *Find a support group.* Support groups—such as parent eduction

classes, community groups, and church-sponsored mother's clubs—offer both information and camaraderie. Full-time mothers can renew each other with sane and silly conversations about their kids.

3. *Keep your brain "tuned up."* One mother started using her personal time to reread her favorite Dickens' classics. It grew into a reading club with her support-group friends. Others keep their minds active with crafts, part-time in-home businesses, or continuing education.

4. *Nurture adult relationships.* Some moms and dads make it a point to go out without the kids once a week to maintain their identity as couples. [It's also a good idea for moms to develop a relationship with a "mother mentor." A women's Bible study is another way to stay in touch with the adult world. As the number of full-time at-home moms grows, so do the places you can connect. Consider a mother's blog, online message boards, websites such as Mamma Said, mySpace, and Homemakers By Choice.]

5. *Don't take yourself too seriously.* Many full-time moms make unreasonable demands on themselves because they don't work outside the home. Overcommitment can be a problem too.

6. *Exercise regularly.* Many moms go to a gym, exercise at home with a video, or attend "Mommy and Me" exercise classes with their children. Others get their exercise by putting their children in the stroller and walking around the block.

7. *Develop a "last gasp" strategy.* It helps to have a plan for days when everything goes wrong. When she crosses the frustration threshold, one mom hires a babysitter and goes shopping. Another takes herself and her child out to lunch. Another hands her son over to her husband when he gets home, then soaks in the bathtub with a magazine.[4]

learn to do what you say you'll do

I often ask the women in my seminars, "How many of you have goals?" Hands wave everywhere. About 90 percent of the women I meet have goals. Then I ask, "How many of you have written down your goals?" Hands drop. Women self-consciously twist their rings or plow through their purses for a breath mint or Kleenex. Only about 10 percent of the women who have goals actually have written them down.

I think we are afraid to write down our goals because putting them in black and white commits us to action. But without a commitment to action you won't grow. You might be interested to know that 80 percent of the people who commit their goals to writing accomplish them, while only 20 percent of those who have goals but don't write them down actually achieve them.

Here's a suggestion to help you get started on personal growth through goal-setting. Select several one-word goals for different areas of your life: your domestic responsibilities, your relationship with your husband, children, and friends, etc. For example, my one-word goal for relating to friends is "slowly," since I'm often so energetic that I leave little room for them. My personal goal for participation in worship is "enthusiasm." My goal for writing this book was "encouragement."

Ask God to help you write a "life phrase"—a goal for your life to be applied in every circumstance. Over 20 years ago I wrote the following phrase (it took me a month to put it together): "To show joy in my life by enthusiastic example, action, teaching, and perseverance." The activities of my life change, but this goal remains.

If you are uncertain about your goals, you might enjoy reading chapter three, the goal-setting chapter, in my book *Secrets to Getting More Done in Less Time*. Think about your goals. Write them down and begin to pray about them, meditate on them, and plan ways to implement them in your experience. You'll be excited as you begin to see yourself grow.

12

your personal places
clothes, closets, correspondence

In addition to making time in your schedule for Bible study, prayer, and personal growth, there are other areas in your personal life as an at-home mom that need your constant attention. As you have probably discovered, there are some things that tend to get away from us if we don't keep them in order. In this chapter I would like to talk to you about four of them: your wardrobe, your schedule, your correspondence, and your future.

dress for your life

I recently had the opportunity to visit with a small group of mothers with young children. They asked me to talk to them about a woman's outward appearance. What can a mom do about maintaining her appearance? Often she has little time or money to invest in how she looks. But they asked some good questions: What should I wear for the activities I'm involved in? How do I decide what kinds of clothes to buy? I spent an hour with them answering their questions. Here are some of the wardrobe tips I offered. Perhaps they will be helpful to you as well.

1. *Dress to exhibit confidence and self-control.* You will feel most

confident about your activities and more in control of your life when you are dressed appropriately for the day. It may be jeans and a T-shirt, slacks and a sweater, a skirt and a shirt, or a dress and heels. Whatever outfit makes you feel in control of yourself for a given occasion, wear it. You will be better prepared to meet the demands of the day when you feel confident about the way you look. "Dress first and fast each day," is an Otto motto. It is a freeing way of life; and you are prepared to go anywhere.

2. *Build your wardrobe around your "activity wheel."* A wardrobe can be a real problem. What should you buy? What should you keep? How do you know if you have too many casual outfits and not enough dressy items?

Consider planning your wardrobe around a wardrobe activity wheel (see diagram on page 128).

View the different activities of your week as the sections of a wheel. The more time you spend in each kind of activity, the larger its section on the wheel will be. Your activity wheel graphically reveals how you spend your time and dictates how you should balance your wardrobe.

For example, let's say that you're a mom with four children still at home. You probably spend the majority of your week in casual clothes. Your wardrobe should be amply stocked with a good selection of comfortable, serviceable clothes for working around the house, taking the children to their activities, etc.

Perhaps you're also committed to exercise and fitness, so a proportionate amount of your wardrobe would be dedicated to specialized clothing for aerobics class (tights, shoes), tennis (shorts, tops, shoes), backpacking (hiking shorts, shirts, boots), etc. You like to get out occasionally to shop and lunch with your friends, so a section of your wheel should be reserved for casual attire. And an appropriate section of your wheel should be designated for those dressy special occasions—church, a fancy dinner out with your husband, a concert, etc. A young friend told me that tight skirts and SUV's don't work well together.

Take a wardrobe inventory occasionally. What do you own? What do you need? When you have some shopping money, compare your activity wheel with the clothes in your closet and dresser. You will be able to quickly discover the areas of your wardrobe that need to be expanded.[1]

3. *Coordinate your wardrobe around your basic colors.* I recommend that you build your wardrobe around the basic colors that work best for you. Make sure all your main pieces are in these colors. This approach makes wardrobe maintenance simple, economical, and time-saving. Yet it allows you to be creative with accessories and feel confident that you are dressed well for every occasion.

I began coordinating my wardrobe 30 years ago. I bought a good black suit because black is one of my best colors. I added black shoes and a black bag, so I didn't have to worry about many other accessories. Next I added a black-and-white tweed skirt that I could wear with my suit jacket. Then I found a red shirt on sale that I could wear with either skirt and the jacket.

Later I bought a coordinating houndstooth suit that increased the mix and match possibilities of my wardrobe. I could interchange the skirts and jackets of both suits. I complemented these outfits with white, wine, and black skirts. Since my activity wheel indicated a need for dressy blouses, I added black and white silky blouses of different styles and a white oxford shirt for casual wear.

If you looked at my wardrobe today you would discover that it's pretty much the same. The styles have changed, but I still dress in the basic colors of black and white. Coordinating your wardrobe around your main colors will greatly increase the variety of your outfits.

You may be thinking, "I don't wear suits. I don't need blazers or jackets in my wardrobe." If you wear sweaters or jackets of any kind, a suit jacket or blazer is just as acceptable, and often will look better. In addition, a jacket becomes the basis of your dress outfit. Consider

WARDROBE ACTIVITY WHEEL

(Circle represents 168 hours)

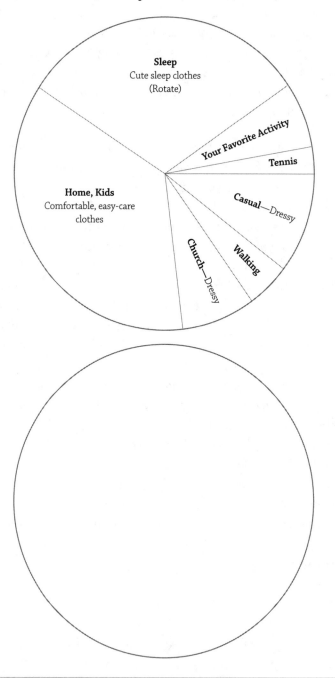

WARDROBE INVENTORY

Blouses   _____   Dresses   _____   Jackets   _____
_____   _____   _____
_____   _____   _____
_____   _____   _____
_____   _____   _____

Shirts   _____   _____   _____
_____   _____   Sweaters   _____
_____   _____   _____
_____   _____   _____
_____   _____   _____

_____   Slacks   _____   _____
_____   _____   _____

Skirts   _____   _____   Accessories   _____
_____   _____   _____
_____   _____   _____
_____   _____   _____

_____   _____   Shoes   _____

Suits   _____   _____   _____
_____   _____   _____
_____   _____   _____
_____   _____   _____
_____   _____   _____

adding a suit to your dress wardrobe, perhaps a three-piece outfit including skirt, slacks, and jacket.

4. *When you feel down, dress up.* Sometimes when I'm lethargic, tired, or discouraged, the simple act of dressing up really gives me a boost. Follow the advice of Dolly in "Hello Dolly" by putting on your Sunday clothes when you feel down and out. Doing something about your outward appearance somehow affects your attitude and emotions. When you're feeling down and dumpy, take a bath or shower, fix your hair, and put on your makeup. Get out of your pajamas and robe, sweats, or grubbies and put on your Sunday best. You'll be surprised at how dressing up can brighten your mood.

5. *Keep an apron between you and the mess.* Have you ever dressed up for the high point of your day or evening only to get your clothes soiled or wrinkled before you leave? For instance, you're doing some last minute dusting before you leave for the PTA meeting, and you inadvertently spray Pledge all over your new slacks. Or you're finishing a family breakfast just before leaving for church when your two-year-old sneezes a mouthful of Froot Loops all over you.

Years ago I discovered the value of aprons, and they have been a wonderful, inexpensive lifesaver to my wardrobe ever since. Early in the day I grab an apron and put it on to protect my outfit of the day. I started out with plain, white bib aprons, then I inherited a few old florals from my grandmother. (Her aprons were all stained around the tummy area where she used to wipe her hands.) Through the years I have collected a number of aprons that are as decorative as they are useful.

Not long ago some dear friends threw a birthday party for me. Knowing me as they do, they made aprons the theme. Each of them wore an apron to the party. They presented an apron fashion show, and each lady told me the story of the apron she wore. Then, best of all, my friends gave me the aprons as birthday gifts! It was a wonderful party, and I received some very special aprons.

Keep some aprons handy to protect your clothes. They will give you the freedom to work around the house without the fear of messing up your outfits. Whenever we eat pasta at our house, just family or family and friends, there is an apron at every chair to protect our clothes.

6. *Don't overlook your bedroom wardrobe.* Often when I discuss wardrobe variety with women's groups, I ask, "How many of you sleep in the same nightgown or pajamas more than three nights in a row?" Large numbers of them giggle nervously and raise their hands. Women who would never wear the same outfit five days in a row often go to bed in the same sleepwear every night of the week.

Think about it: You spend about one-third of your entire life in sleepwear. Why not give the same careful attention to your bedroom wardrobe as to your public wardrobe? Do it for yourself. Do it for your husband and children. Save up and get four or five different sets of pajamas or gowns. Make them as cute as possible. Wear a different one each night, wash them after a few wearings, and rotate them again the next week.

7. *Don't forget your inner appearance.* Anne Ortlund encourages women never to spend more time on outward appearance than on inward appearance. Her encouragement is in line with 1 Peter 3:3-4: "Let not your adornment be merely external—braiding the hair, and wearing gold jewelry, and putting on dresses; but let it be the hidden person of the heart, with the imperishable quality of a gentle and quiet spirit, which is precious in the sight of God." Anne says that the Proverbs 31 woman, who is often referred to as the model wife and mother, focuses on inner qualities: "Twenty-two verses describe this woman's kindness, goodness, hard work, loving relationships—and only one verse out of 22 describes how she looked. But she looked simply great!"[2] It was this insight that prompted Anne to practice spending $1/_{22}$ of her time on outer beauty and $21/_{22}$ on inner beauty. She has her priorities in order!

8. *Make the most of your closet space.* How does your closet look? Do

you want to organize your closet to keep it neat, orderly, and efficient for wardrobe storage? Here's an idea for revamping your closet.

In the section of the closet where you hang your shirts, blouses, and jackets, remount the hanger rod high enough to allow space for another row of clothes to hang below. Then drop a length of chain from the middle and each end of the rod, and attach a sturdy wooden dowel to them. This gives you more space to hang shirts and jackets.

Do the same in the section where your husband keeps his shirts and jackets. Keep one or two sections of the hanger rod at its original height for hanging slacks and dresses.

Also consider attaching racks, chains, and dowels to the backs of the doors in bathrooms, bedrooms, and linen closets. This will give you extra storage space for towels, accessories, tomorrow's clothes, etc.

the days of your life

One of the most effective tools for ordering your personal life is an organizing/planning notebook. Organizers help women keep track of appointments, anniversaries, birthdays, and even a husband's business schedule. An organizer can help you keep your growing, busy family on schedule.

I recommend a personal organizer that is expandable. It should have rings that allow you to insert and remove sheets. Your organizer should at least include a month-at-a-glance calendar, important phone numbers and addresses, and blank paper for notes and journal entries. Stay away from spiral-bound notebooks. They cannot grow and adapt with you.

To make effective use of an organizer, you must be willing to write and read. I'm not kidding. You must faithfully write dates, events, and times in your organizer, and then be sure to read them! The information you store on the pages of your organizer is only helpful if you read those pages regularly.

Carry your organizer wherever you go. "Oh, Donna," you say,

"I already carry a purse and a diaper bag. How can I possibly carry something else?"

Get a larger bag and combine some of those things. When your children are small, your primary travel necessities are not personal grooming articles. You're loaded down with diapers, a change of clothing, formula, baby wipes, bottles for water or juice, food, and bibs. So you need a big bag for the baby. Just make sure the bag is big enough for you to add your wallet, a tube of lipstick, and your organizer. They'll all fit.

When the baby isn't with you, slip your organizer into a large purse or carry it under your arm.

write when you can

I love to write letters, which has really become a lost art even though we all love to read letters. Years ago David said to me, "No matter what happens in life, no matter what our economic situation becomes, no matter how much the cost of postage stamps goes up, keep writing!" I must have written some dandy letters to him in the past to make him carry on like that. So I write letters regularly. Do you?

A very dear friend of mine lost her parents within a few months of each other. As my friend was sorting through her mom's personal possessions she found a stack of old letters. Some of them had been written by a soldier who was overseas during World War II to his wife at home, who was pregnant at that time with the infant who would grow up to become my friend.

My friend discovered that her father's letters to her mother were filled with words of love for her and anticipation for the future and how they would raise their firstborn child together. As my friend read her father's words, she was so affirmed in the relationship she had enjoyed with her parents. "I'm so glad I found these letters," she told me later. "How precious and permanent is the written word."

It's important to maintain relationships with our loved ones through notes and letters. But like so many other things we should do and want to do, personal correspondence is seen as an elephant-like task we don't have time for. But if you make it a priority, you can consume this elephant one brief letter at a time.

For example, perhaps you live a great distance from your mother. You know she would love to receive a note each week. So why not write her a letter by jotting one paragraph a day. By the end of the week you have a letter full of interesting family news.

When I used to write letters this way, I kept a notepad next to the sheet of stationery on which I was composing a letter to a friend. Whenever something happened that I thought she'd like to know about, I jotted a couple of words on the notepad that would help me remember it. Perhaps it was something adorable that Anissa did that I wished my friend had been here for. Later, when I had a few minutes, I sat down and wrote the details of the items I had scribbled on my pad. The length of each letter depended on my homefront needs.

If the expense of postage is a problem for your budget, suggest that your out-of-town loved ones buy a roll or two of stamps for your birthday or Christmas present. They'll be glad to oblige. And knowing they've sent you all those stamps will give you the perseverance to keep on writing.

E-mail has been a boost to relationships. From finding a mate to group newsletters, use your computer to get in touch with and stay connected to people. E-notes, e-greeting cards, photos, videos...technology has made amazing strides in helping us stay in touch. Why, I can even sing to my grandchild over the internet!

conclusion

A few years ago, I was wrapping a package for mailing. That fat, very sticky tape was sticking to everything but the box it was intended for. I was annoyed, but suddenly I thought the tape reminded me of myself. I was sticking to places I did not want to be sticking to, and not "sticking it out" with what I knew God had planned. That day I took a 3 x 5 card and stuck a piece of tape on the front with the phrases, "Do what you can do" and "Do it now." It was a friendly, funny reminder for me to be a woman with stick-to-itiveness...or perseverance.

Ordering your personal life is primarily a spiritual matter. Isaiah 26:3 reads: "You will keep him in perfect peace, whose mind is stayed on You, because he trusts in You" (NKJV). I pray that you will experience daily the peace that comes from centering your mind on Christ and ordering your personal life to please Him.

13

supporting your man

The day you said "I do" you chose your love;
since then you have been learning to love
your choice.

Some years ago I was asked to provide a brief lesson at a bridal shower. As I pondered what I might say, the concept of the bridal veil came to mind. I made a simple veil from a puffy piece of netting, some white flowers, and lace. When it was time for the lesson, I placed the homemade veil on the head of the bride-to-be and shared a few words of encouragement with her concerning the important step she was about to take.

I reminded her that the bridal veil symbolized her passage from protected innocence to commitment to one special man. As the ceremony begins, the bride belongs to the first man in her life, her father, who proudly escorts her down the aisle. But at the altar he relinquishes her to another man, the groom. After the officiant pronounces the couple husband and wife, the beaming groom lifts the veil for their first kiss as a married couple. And the bride willingly grants him access to her lips and, "till death do us part," to her entire life.

I talked about the parallel between the bridal veil and the veil in the tabernacle between the holy place and the holy of holies (discussed in the Old Testament). For centuries the tabernacle veil separated God from His people except for one day each year (the Day of Atonement) when the high priest was allowed to enter to offer sacrifice for himself and the nation of Israel. But when Christ died on the cross, the veil was torn from top to bottom (see Matthew 27:51), symbolizing the complete access we now have to God through Christ (see Hebrews 10:19-22). Similarly, when the bridal veil is lifted, the bride offers to her groom complete access, which was not available to him before they said "I do."

As I concluded my talk, I lifted the veil and said, "Ruthie, when your new husband lifts this veil on your wedding day, remember that you gave him permission to do so. Through your marriage commitment you grant him total and permanent access to your life, emotionally and physically. As your marriage goes on, there will be times, dear, sweet Ruthie, when even you won't want to share something with your husband or when an argument disrupts your relationship. You will be tempted to pull down the veil and separate yourself from him. Don't do it. Once the veil is lifted, it is gone forever. You are totally his." Then I gave Ruthie a small, square piece of netting as a reminder of the lesson of the lifted veil.

Whether you wore a veil on your wedding day or not, I invite you to consider its symbolism in your relationship to your husband. Through your marriage vows, you and your husband became one. On that precious day, perhaps many years ago, you granted him complete access to your life. Next to your relationship with God, nurturing your relationship with that one special man is the most important responsibility you have. Your understanding of the concepts of complete accessibility, entrance, and surrender are essential to your success as an at-home wife and mom.

getting to know him

My husband, David, is a gift of God's loving provision to me, and I am God's gift to him. But after many years of marriage, I'm still learning about the wonderful gift I received when I lifted my veil and welcomed him into my life. I remember David telling me early in our marriage, "The hardest task you will face being married to me is really getting to know me." I thought, *What are you talking about? I already know you very well.* But over the years I came to understand what he was saying.

Like most of us, David is a complicated person. And, as a man, he's not as verbal as most women—and he's certainly not as verbal as I am! (Gary Smalley claims that men speak about 12,000 words per day while women speak about 25,000 words per day. David is sure I can hit 45,000 on a good day!) Often I found that I couldn't tell what he was thinking. As he predicted, one of my greatest tasks has been getting to really know him.

I encourage you to do absolutely everything you can to discover who your husband is, why he does what he does, and how he arrives at the decisions he makes in his life. Learn to draw him out by asking good questions and being a good listener. Learn also to demonstrate your gratefulness for who he is and what he does. Show your appreciation in tangible ways with expressions of physical affection. In front of the children, kiss him on the cheek, squeeze his hand, and speak to him lovingly and kindly. In private, show your affection in more intimate, physical ways.

Demonstrate your support for your husband by agreeing with him and, if agreement is not possible, surrendering your will cheerfully. Learn to understand why he makes the choices he makes and then support him in those choices.

You may be thinking that I make it sound pretty easy. Oh, I know it's not always easy. I think that's why Paul wrote to Titus about the older women teaching the younger women how to love their husbands and children (see Titus 2:3,4). Interesting concept, isn't it, that you and I need to be taught how to love our husbands? In those early days of romantic love I didn't think for one moment that I needed to be taught how to love David. Yet I have discovered as you have (or will) that learning to know, love, and support your husband is a process that is necessary for making a good marriage. The day you said "I do" you chose your love; since then you have been learning to love your choice.

There are times when David and I feel so connected that we're sure we could sit down at the breakfast table and come up with a plan to resolve all the troubles in the world. There are other times, of course, when we feel so disconnected that all he has to do is ask me where his favorite mug is and I think he's criticizing how I store the dishes.

Over the years of your commitment to your husband there will be times when you don't feel connected to him. Whether or not you feel connected, you are still committed.

One day David and I were having a disagreement about something, and I started to cry. The issue was not resolved, nor did we yet know how it was going to be resolved. But he walked across the room and tenderly said to me, "Just remember: I am committed to you." Commitment is the first step to true intimacy.

The issue was painful, and we still had to work it through. But there was a great sense of relief knowing that no matter what, David was committed to me. It's important that we learn to verbalize our loving commitment to our husbands, especially in times of disagreement and conflict.

opposites attract

Knowing and loving your man includes being willing to recognize and celebrate your differences. Your personality styles and many of your interests and tastes are different. Allow your personality traits to complement each other. Make your differences assets to your marriage.

If you knew us, you'd say David and I are quite different. Are we ever! He is quiet. I rarely am. He is able to do fine detailed work and concentrate on it for long periods of time. Not me! He is very coordinated and athletic. I'm not. I love butter; he hates it. He drinks his coffee black; I need cream and sugar. He's analytical; I'm emotional. Our differences provide lots of opportunities for conflict. And yet, over the years, we have learned to recognize and celebrate our differences and make them work for us instead of against us.

Here's an example. When we buy a car, we get a previously owned one because we believe we get better value for our money. We also pay cash to avoid paying interest. When it's time to buy another car, analytical David does the research, decides on the model and year, and locates possible cars to buy. We discuss the price range we can live with. Then I take over and work out a deal with the potential seller. I'm a trader and negotiator at heart. By working together David and I get the car we want at the price we want.

living with another human being

I received the following anonymous quote from a mother: "Why are some men so smart, neat, caring, and helpful until they become husbands? Probably for the same reason some women are so smart, neat, caring, and helpful until they become wives." She added this note: "I posted this on my refrigerator to bring me back to reality when I get pompous about my husband's faults!"

It sure is easy for us to look at our husbands and wish they would change. Recently I chatted informally with a small group of mothers at a women's retreat where I was speaking. A number of them admitted how tough it was being married to their husbands. As they began to list their husbands' faults, I stopped them and told them something I heard Elisabeth Elliot say. I'll never forget her standing before 500 women and saying in her frightfully cultured voice, "You've married a sinner." She paused, and the women grew noticeably enthusiastic about the idea. Just about the time the audience was convinced that their husbands were the problem, Elisabeth added, "And he married one too!"

How easy it is for us to blame our husbands for lack of moral support and for not appreciating the sacrifices we make raising children and keeping a home. Yes, we married sinners. But we need to remember that we are just as guilty of imperfection as they are. They married sinners too!

Be careful to support your husband in his spiritual development instead of criticizing him when he's not as saintly as you would prefer. Consider the situation. One of your greatest needs in a marriage relationship is for financial support and security. Your husband works hard to make it possible for you to stay at home and to provide the security you need. You are able to attend Bible studies and take time during your day to read God's Word and listen to encouraging, affirming Christian broadcasts. You have a greater opportunity for continuing spiritual education than your husband does because he spends his days at work.

This doesn't mean that your husband is less spiritual than you are. His work may give him a great many opportunities for exercising and developing his spirituality. He just may not have the same access to resources that you have.

I can remember being disappointed because David didn't bury his nose in God's Word and attend Bible studies. I eventually realized that one of the most spiritual things he did on a daily basis was to faithfully commit himself to a job that provided for me an opportunity to be at home. Perhaps you have that privilege or seek it. If so, pray for your husband. Pray for the work he does. And be careful that you don't demand too much of him spiritually. Instead, support him in his spiritual ministry of hard work. He will grow spiritually, and so will you.

Another fact is that as an at-home wife, you will have opportunities to promote your husband's career and even help advance it. You are a strategic asset to him.

As you support your husband, remember that your children are watching. Your son is learning from you by the "catch it" method what kind of wife he should choose. Do you want him to find a wife that will do him "good and not evil all the days of her life"

(Proverbs 31:12)? Then you must model that behavior as you support his father spiritually and in every other way.

supportive suggestions

You have probably read a book or two about how you can meet your husband's needs and build a good marriage. I don't hope to duplicate in these next few pages the excellent advice found in scores of Christian books on marriage. But I do have a few ideas about how you can support the man who works so hard so you can be an at-home mom.

1. *Keep an orderly household.* A man desires to have his home, meals, and children maintained in an organized way. He may not often say so, but he does. I speak to women frequently on the subject of having an organized, efficient home. Some women tell me their husbands don't really care about an orderly home, that they don't mind the mess. But when I have an opportunity to speak to men, or when they write to me, few tell me they don't mind the mess. The majority say they desire to have a home that is run efficiently and well.

They talk about wanting a home that is organized so they can find things when they need them. They talk about wanting a place of rest and quiet. The old line that a man's home is his castle seems to be more than just a saying. Men want to come home to a place of peace and restoration. They also like meals at home; don't forget the way to a man's heart is through his stomach.

Just because your husband won't talk about it doesn't mean that he doesn't desire or appreciate domestic support. Since most men are not as verbal as women, they are not always able to articulate the stress they face daily in their work environment. If you work or have worked, you may understand his situation somewhat, but probably not completely. In your inability to fully understand the pressures your man faces, you need to provide an enormous support system at home.

The husband in Proverbs 31 gives his wife charge over many things: the slaves, the property, meal preparation. She takes her responsibility seriously, not grudgingly. She does everything possible to support her husband and make his life more comfortable so he can serve God better. Like the Proverbs 31 woman, many women today find that their relationships with their husband, children, and friends are all enhanced when each of the people involved has an abiding walk with God.

There's a cycle here. God gives the husband headship in the household. The husband assigns part of that responsibility to his wife. The wife accomplishes her tasks so that her husband might have more time to be restored and draw closer to God. As he does, he is free to take care of his wife. Do yourself a favor by providing an orderly home for your husband.

2. *Institute a "home free" policy.* Another of a man's desires is for periods of quiet. As I think about the early days of our marriage, David really never had a quiet, peaceful place for himself. He got up early, prepared himself for work, went to the office, and came home to an evening of family, friends, and church commitments. Or there was work around the house to be done: mowing the lawn, maintaining the cars, etc. Then off we'd go to bed so we could get up and start all over again.

As a young mother I began to cherish the minutes of quiet I was able to grab for myself in the comfortable surroundings of my own home. When I realized how important these times were for my restoration, I was much more eager to provide periods of quiet and restoration for David.

So we developed a "home free" policy. When a child touches home base in a game of tag, he is home free, safe from others who are chasing him. Similarly, when David arrived home from work, I made sure he was home free. He got a hug and a kiss, of course, and heard the exciting events of Anissa's day. But then he was home free for 30 minutes. If kids were in the house making a commotion, they had to be quiet during David's home-free period. He could change his clothes, read his paper, have a snack, sit outdoors, or do whatever would help him restore his quiet and unrushed spirit.

Even now, when the house is empty of children and there are

just the two of us, I do my best to provide a place of quiet for David. I try not to be on the phone or have people over when he arrives home. And it works! Soon David is in the kitchen and we talk about the day.

3. *Put your man first.* When I was about 27 years old, a wise woman said to me, "Your daughter will only be with you for about 20 years, but your husband will always be there. Always put him before your children." Well, she was right. Anissa has long since left home, but David is still here. Our close relationship continues on.

Let nothing come between you and your husband—not your house, not your pride, not your friends, not your work, not your kids. You and your husband are one. The children will be there, of course. They are part of you, and you are responsible for them. But there is no relationship on earth like the marriage relationship. It is so important that God uses it as a model for the church (see Ephesians 5:22-33). Nurture your relationship with your husband so that it lasts the longest and means the most.

4. *Live sacrificially.* A mom said to me, "Why do I have to make all the sacrifices in our marriage?" In fact, she wasn't making all the sacrifices. No marriage partner makes all the sacrifices. At that moment she simply felt like she was. And yet sacrifice is a very real part of a wife and mother's role.

Sacrifice is something most women understand. We sacrificed our autonomy when we married. We gave up our maiden names (most of us). We sacrificed our privacy when we surrendered access to our husbands physically and emotionally. We sacrificed our bodies to have children, and some of us never recovered physically! (I still have stretch marks!)

Being a wife is a life of sacrifice. Understand, however, that Christ has called us to this life. His was a life of sacrifice. He asks us to follow His example in our ministry to our husbands and children (see Philippians 2:3-5).

When I talk about living sacrificially, some women respond, "I would agree with you about sacrifice if I had married the right man. But I married the wrong man. I married a man who is too different from me, a man my parents opposed, a man who has not chosen Christ." Perhaps you are saying this about your marriage relationship.

I understand the pain of such an experience. But I am also confident that the sacrifices you make to serve your husband will be valuable to you. We cannot look down the road at any point in life and see how the future is going to turn out. But God can. He knows the beginning from the end, and He will give you the strength to surrender and sacrifice in your marriage.

But what if you're not married? What if you are widowed or divorced? In her book *Mommy, Where Are You?* Kathi Mills addressed this issue. "Whether you're widowed, divorced, or never married, that Scripture in Isaiah 54 ['For your Maker is your husband'] applies to you. In fact, if you're a single-parent father, it applies to you too. If you will let Him, he will be a husband to you. He will love you and care for you and provide for you in ways you never imagined."

5. *Send him off in the morning with breakfast and support.* His breakfast may just be coffee and your smiling supportive face. Also receive him at the end of the day by stopping what you are doing to welcome him home.

6. *Study your ever-changing husband.* While your husband may not work in a hostile environment, he certainly faces the pressures of a post-Christian country. And most likely he works in a non-Christian workplace. In fact, even Christian workplaces have their stress points. Consider the effects of the environment your husband faces every day. Pray for him; be kind to him.

When he comes home, make sure he feels supported as a man, a husband, a father, and a fellow believer in Jesus Christ. Demonstrate your support by creating an environment in which he can rest, relax, reveal himself, and restore himself. His constant provision for your family in financial, emotional, and spiritual ways is a daily blessing. In return, be the comfort and support God has called you to be in his life.

your man is not your enemy

The laundry is ready for washing (almost), the dishes are soaking in the sink, the to-do list is ready for the day, and you even know what you are going to make for dinner. For the moment it is quiet in the house and you have the opportunity to think. While I know this is not a frequent state of being, I also know for the full-time, at-home mom there are occasional moments to think about bigger things beyond the pesky routines of life. As one of our primary relationships, marriage is often where our thoughts turn, frequently focusing on our husbands.

I also know that, as a stay-at-home mom, it is easy to perseverate on problems. There is one person who frequently stands at the center of our problems and it certainly isn't us. It's *him!* You know, the guy you married.

- He who leaves his socks on the floor.
- He who puts his glass in the sink even though the dishwasher is only inches away.
- He who did not help you bathe the children or tuck them into bed last night (again)!
- He who does not talk to you enough and yet knows where to find you at bedtime.

Yes, that's the "him"—your husband—and despite some evidence to the contrary, he is *not* the enemy.

When David and I were planning our wedding, we had the good sense to enter into premarital counseling for 12 weeks. I am sure it was great, but the only piece of advice we now recall receiving was the pastor looking at me and saying "Remember, Donna, he is not the enemy." For good measure, he then turned to my handsome husband-to-be and repeated: "David, remember, she is not the enemy."

At the time, we thought it mildly helpful but not particularly relevant. After all, we were in love! It was a nice piece of advice from the pastor, but nothing more. Of course, our mate-to-be was not the enemy. That was so obvious, we thought.

Time passed...and wouldn't you know, one day several years later I found myself furious with my husband. We were in the middle of a verbal war, and David was totally responsible. I remember saying aloud, "This is a war zone and if you want a fight, I'm coming with a battle plan." I was a little dramatic and drew on my avid interest in World War II, which made me an expert on such things as battle plans and warfare.

But God intervened. At that very moment I remembered the pastor's words. You know: "Remember, Donna, he is not the enemy." My next thought was, *Well, if David's not, he certainly bears a striking resemblance to the enemy. He's looking and acting like one.*

An enemy is one that is antagonistic to another, who wishes the other harm. An enemy is someone who wants to overthrow or confound his opponent. An enemy is a hostile force. And hostility certainly fit this situation. In my case, David is a lawyer and confounding the other side is what he does for a living.

But when the dust cleared and I looked at David and thought of the definitions of "enemy," I knew he wasn't one, even if at times it felt like it. If David was not the enemy, then who was? And what was the battleground for this fight?

The real enemy of marriage is the same enemy who has power in this world. He has power now but will not always. This enemy seeks to destroy what God has created and called His own. The enemy is spoken of in Scripture as Satan. Yes, that enemy. Please hear me out. Believers in Christ know that there is and always has been a war against God's plan. Marriage is a core part of God's plan. We stand against the enemy when we choose marriage over other relationship plans.

Satan is still loose and still has power in the world—and that power wants to interrupt relationships that honor God. But the enemy does not have unlimited power. Those who choose to serve God and desire to obey His word have superior force through Jesus Christ.

If winning or losing is a regular issue in your marriage, there's help available. Let's examine the real enemy and what is at stake. This will help you fight using the proper ammunition. It will also help you recognize your allies in this battle and the armor that is available to you. We all will have issues in marriage, but God's plan is for the marriage to not just survive, but to prosper.

When you marry you are enlisting for life. You are saying before a large or small gathering, "I will make my yes be yes; I will not allow anything to put this vow aside." What you committed to was closing the exits and refusing to allow yourself any alternatives except working out difficult situations in your marriage. God uses marriage as a testimony to His mercy and grace, and that testimony reaches your children and others.

Please remember that no one made you marry this man. It was your choice. When we look at God's plan for marriage we see several main points:

1. Two shall become one.[1]
2. They shall find pleasure in one another and propagate the earth.[2]
3. He shall love, protect, and provide for her.[3]
4. She shall respect, admire, and support him.[4]
5. They shall be inseparable.[5]
6. Each shall gain a clearer understanding of grace.

7. The world shall see what marriage to Christ is like.

8. They shall together glorify God.

As we come together as husband and wife, our relationship is a living testimony to and about God. People see something of God in a marriage based on His principles and plan. There are three parties to a marriage, and I am not referring to your mother-in-law. The three are:

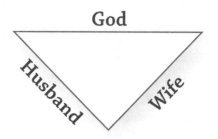

Each person has a pivotal role in winning the war the enemy and our current culture sets against marriage. There can be no godly marriage without these three properly handling their roles. God is the top of this triangle. His Word proclaims, "The Lord Our God, the Lord is one, love the Lord your God with all your heart and with all your soul and with all your strength" (Mark 12:29 ESV).

God calls the husband to be the head of this union called marriage: "For the husband is the head of the wife even as Christ is the head of the church" (Ephesians 5:23 ESV). The husband is to love his wife, sacrificially and treat her as kindly as he would his own body. He is to grant his wife honor (1 Peter 3:7).

God calls the wife to respect her husband and be subject to him: "Wives, submit to your own husband as to the Lord" (1 Peter 3:1 ESV).

In the army there are officers and rules. In a marriage it's the same. The Bible gives us the rules and how to follow each rule. In the military, soldiers are "told what to do" and no matter what they think, the entire battalion works best when they adhere to the rules.

Following the military model, God has assigned each of us specific tasks to accomplish:

Major Players	Primary Task
Husband	Love
Wife	Submit
Children	Obey
Parents	Do not exacerbate (provoke) your children

How we fulfill those roles can vary quite a lot, but the overall principles remain. The important thing to remember is that you and your husband are on the same side and on the same team.

And don't misunderstand me. The wife is to submit, but that doesn't mean she doesn't actively participate in the decision-making and life of the marriage. For instance, in David's and my marriage, our key goal is agreement. David and I talk, wait, pray, consider, and reconsider before the "card of submission" is played. Even then, I *choose* to submit. David cannot force me to bend his way. This healthy submission directly contrasts with toxic submission, which includes not speaking, not helping, not sharing your heart or hurts, violence of any kind, and submitting to your husband with discontent and/or anger.

When I was a young, impressionable woman, I remember hearing a conference leader say "No one likes to be told what to do." The speaker caught my attention, and since then I have found situation after situation where someone who is being told what to do doesn't like it. The person rebels. Rebellion in the troops is painful and must be corrected with the authority God offers. Living by this principle will help you and your husband get along so well. Let me say it again. *No one likes to be told what to do!*

when trouble comes

Every marriage encounters difficulties. When trouble arises between you and your spouse, we can turn to God's Word again for advice. Going back to our military example, soldiers need armor and ammunition as defensive cover. The apostle Paul tells us to put on the whole armor of God so we can stand against the schemes of the devil (see Ephesians 6). Not just one piece of the armor but the whole armor:

- Belt of truth
- Breastplate of righteousness
- Shoes of peace
- Shield of faith
- Helmet of salvation
- Word of the Spirit

Armor is a defensive covering. When disagreements arise, use your best defenses, such as thinking before you speak, speaking softly, not crying or screaming, biting your tongue, and knowing your man.

In all "wars," each side has the option to call a truce. A truce is not admitting defeat; it just buys time and gives people space to rest, contemplate, and plan. Ever notice how battles break out at inopportune moments, like Sunday morning or Christmas Eve—just before company arrives? In our house, it's sure to be tense just before David and I speak publicly on marriage. The enemy likes to wound us at times when God is or is going to be proclaimed within or without the family.

I am proposing that you and your husband discuss a truce concept *before* a battle breaks out. Agree in advance that during any battle either of you may declare a truce for an agreed period of time, and that the battle will then cease immediately. Each person will honor the truce.

This has worked so well for our marriage. David usually wants to end the battle before I do. And I want to be sure we don't abandon discussion of the issue by declaring a truce, so the truce includes a promise to discuss the issue again as soon as the down time is over. Then we approach the subject again, only more calmly, after some rest, reflection, and hopefully, prayer. This creates a win–win situation. With time and space each of you will see more clearly and often the squabble that could have turned into a full scale war is averted. The enemy loses, not your marriage. Diplomats use truces to stop hostilities and so can you. A truce doesn't solve things, but it does save things.

Battles will come. Don't be surprised. Be prepared. Be intentional. You probably married a man who is your opposite. Opposites can attack, not just attract. So expect a battle, but understand the marriage is not at stake—just the current issue. Pressures from extended family will arrive. Expect problems. Financial needs will escalate. Expect problems. With each battle we have an opportunity to fight together and present a united front against the outside. Even through disagreements we can take ground for God.

It's true we contribute to the battle out of our own interests and weaknesses. The opponents in this war can be each other, especially when we submit to temptation and behave as the real enemy would like us to behave. The battleground is often right in your home, in the midst of your family, on a stage in front of your children. But it's your choice. How are you reflecting God?

Put on your armor, ladies. God has already won the final battle. Go out and fight for what matters most. Behave as if your husband is your hero. Work to support your ally. Remember, your man is *not* your enemy.

your home, your nest

Home—a place to embrace and be welcomed.

A few years ago I noticed a mother bird building her springtime nest in a corner of our patio. I was concerned that she was too close to the house, so I immediately began to "mother" my new patio companion: "Don't you realize how much noise the Otto household makes and how many interruptions your new family is going to face?" As it turned out, the mother bird was completely unruffled by our presence.

As I sipped coffee, watered plants, or read on the patio over the next few days, I observed this mother bird feathering her nest—a bit of this, a bit of that, here a twig, there a puff of dried dandelion. She reminded me of the way I putter and putz in my home, constantly changing (meeting the needs of our changing lives), rearranging, and making the house more comfortable, more workable, more pleasing to its inhabitants, more inviting to my guests.

What's your priority for your home? To keep it attractive? To keep it (ugh!) clean? To keep a path cleared between the kitchen and the living room? Let me suggest a more reasonable, attainable goal for your nest. Keep your nest in order. Order is something short of squeaky clean but a lot better than chaos. Order allows important family activities to happen in the home, such as family fun and meals. Order is the comfortable predictability of family events, such as breakfast at seven o'clock and dinner at five o'clock. Clean clothes are in the closet, and important papers can actually be located when needed. That's order. Dust and order can coexist for awhile, but only for awhile. I know this isn't always possible, but develop a schedule that works for you and your family.

Order is a gift to yourself and your family. You know what a lack of organization and order does to you, how it wearies and distracts you? Did you ever consider what an impact it has on the young impressionable minds in your home? Lack of order trains children to be disorderly and scattered. It often breeds confusion and frustration in them. But kids generally respond well to orderly predictability in the home. It's comforting to them.

Order in the home results when parents—especially mothers— exert a measure of personal sacrifice and discipline. Anything a mom desires to bring to her children in the way of truth, teaching, or responsibility is usually accomplished at some cost, some sacrifice and discipline. Order in the home is a reflection of that discipline.

order through simplicity

Simplicity helps us keep order. Our world is not a simple place. Complexity and confusion abound. Do you want to buy a cell phone or iPod? How many brands and sizes are there? Think about the variety in the world of computers. And by the time you buy one and figure out how it works, there's a newer generation available.

Do you need a gallon of milk? There's nonfat, one percent, two percent, whole milk, goat's milk, buttermilk—take your pick. We have an abundance of choices every day. Nothing seems simple in our world. If we're going to move toward order in our homes, we're going to have to make some choices for a simpler lifestyle.

A young woman who lives with her husband and three children

in a very small house in southern California describes a simple way of life. Because of the size of the house and their choice of lifestyle, Beth's home is kept very simple. They have no separate playroom, so the children play in the living room. Beth has some rules for simplicity to help keep order. Large toys are not allowed in the living room. Books are allowed and can be piled anywhere—and they are!

Beth describes a wonderful time her oldest son Nathan had one day. He dragged his baby brother's bathtub to the middle of the living room. He wadded up scraps of paper to look like fish and threw them in and around the tub. Then he jumped in and looked gleefully at his mother. "Look, Mommy. I've been fishing, and my boat is full of fish." In their simple way of life, a bathtub became a toy.

I'm not saying that you should move into a smaller home or stop buying toys for your children. But the simpler your lifestyle becomes, the easier it will be for you to keep up.

how to create order

"Okay, Donna," you may be saying, "where I live clothes are piled everywhere. Toys litter every room in the house. Papers are stacked on the kitchen counter and the bureau in the bedroom. The sink is always stacked with dirty dishes. The pantry is a mess. And the refrigerator hasn't been cleaned in a year. Where do I begin?"

Here are two simple steps for creating order out of the chaos in your home.

1. *Get it looking in order.* I call this surface cleaning. Get the biggest box (or boxes or sturdy trash bags) you can find. Take the box through the house and pick up everything that is covering your surface spaces. Toys go into the box. Sheets of paper that need to be sorted go into a paper bag, then into the box. Dirty clothes go into the box to be dropped off when you pass the laundry room. Then go back through the house checking the surface areas you may not have seen in months, making sure they look in order. Feather dust the surface spaces.

If it's been awhile since your house was in order, going through the entire house like this may be a huge job. Remember one of the Ottos' mottos: You can eat an entire elephant if you take it one bite at a time. If you can't surface clean the whole house at one time, do one room at a time by filling a box with everything that is out of order. Eventually you will have your chaos confined to boxes and bags, and the house will have an appearance of order. If you've done all this and still feel you need suggestions for cleaning and organization, you might be encouraged by my book *Secrets to Getting More Done in Less Time*. Don't despair. You can do it!

A surface cleaning will do wonders for your spirit and give you encouragement for getting your home really in order.

2. *Throw away, give away, put away.* Home builders and developers say that only 10 to 15 percent of the space in a home or apartment is designed to be used for active storage. Often, however, because of our desire to save things and our poor storage habits, as much as 35 percent of our home is crammed with stuff. This is not only disorderly and uncomfortable, it's often a fire or safety hazard to have our homes so cluttered.

Here's a plan to help you declare war on the mess in your home. Take three large trash bags into a room you have already surface cleaned. One bag is for stuff to be thrown away, another is for things to be given away, and the third is for items to be put away in another room or to store in the garage or attic. Start with the box of things you collected during your surface cleaning. Everything in the box either goes into one of the three bags or is returned to its proper place in that room.

After you have sorted through the box, go through the entire room the same way. Every item in the room should be either thrown away, given away, or put away properly. Move through every room in the house armed with your three bags. Take a month to do so if necessary (the average house takes 5 to 10 hours of work).

When you fill a throw-away bag, get rid of it quickly so you won't be tempted to keep some of the stuff. When you fill a give-away bag, donate it to a charitable organization which can use the items or sell them in their thrift shop. Items from the put-away bag will be returned to the areas of the house where they belong or be stored.[1]

(We'll talk about setting up a cheap, effective storage system later in the chapter.)

clutter—the enemy of order

The enemy of order is clutter. Clutter, clutter, clutter. Yet I can hear some of you moaning: "Donna, I know my house is cluttered with stuff I don't really need, but it's so hard for me to throw away or give away my possessions." Do you know why? There are a couple of big reasons.

First, many of us were nurtured by parents and grandparents who lived through the Great Depression of the early 1930s. The desperate financial struggles of those years caused drastic changes in people's lives and lifestyles. Some never really recovered from that experience.

If your relatives are anything like mine, you probably grew up hearing statements like, "You better not throw that away; you never know when you'll need it." Or you heard the more subtle but guilt-laden, "You're not going to throw that away, are you?" Or it was, "I'll take that if you're not going to keep it." As a result, some of us grew up trained to save everything. We call ourselves pack rats, but in reality we just have a hard time making decisions.

We left home with our little bundle of treasures, except for some of us the bundle wasn't so little. We got married and our husband's treasures were added to the pile. And the pile just keeps getting bigger. Because of our Depression-tainted upbringing, we can't bear to part with anything.

Second, our homes are cluttered because we see our possessions through an emotional filter. Our stuff may be practically useless or worthless, but it has sentimental value to us. If we kept everything we had some feelings about, we'd never throw anything away!

Let me give you a personal example of how the emotional filter works. I'm of Italian and Persian heritage. I was five feet six inches tall by the seventh grade and skinny—89 pounds—until I was 19. I had bushy, curly hair, and my mom gave me permanents. I wore very plain clothes, and I wasn't allowed to shave my legs. And I have an Italian nose—or maybe I should say Roman. At any rate, it's big!

But when the time came for my 10-year high school reunion, I wasn't so bad looking. In fact, I was pretty cute! I was up to 103 pounds, my hair was no longer curly, and I had learned to shave my legs! (P.S. Don't worry, the skinny days are long gone!)

So to look my very best for the reunion, I spent a little more time and money than I normally would shopping for my dress. It was worth it. My gray dress and I were a hit! I received a lot of affirmation and kind words about my appearance from people I hadn't seen in 10 years.

In the months that followed, every time I wore that dress I remembered how great I felt at my 10-year reunion. So I wore the dress a lot during the next few years! However, after eight years I wasn't wearing it at all. Yet every time I pulled it out of my closet, my emotional filter kicked in. That dress was special. But it hung in my closet unworn, a closet that could become very disorderly if I hung onto every item I was emotionally attached to.

When you understand your pack-rat heritage and your emotional attachment to things, you should be able to handle more easily the discipline of parting with what you don't need. If you haven't used it or worn it in two years, get rid of it. If it doesn't fit you, get rid of it. If it's a color you don't wear, get rid of it.

Sometimes you need an outsider who does not have your emotional filter to help you sort through your "treasures." A friend of mine looked at that eight-year-old gray dress and said, "Dump it; it's a dog."

One rule to help reduce clutter at Christmastime is "Christmas in, Christmas out." If 10 new items come into your house or wardrobe as gifts, send 10 other items out by throwing them away or giving them away.

We keep accumulating things, and during the Christmas season it seems to get worse. If there is no outflow, over time the clutter becomes pretty sizable. More is not always better. The Western world is awakening to our ecological responsibilities. Much of what we acquire and accumulate has an environmental price tag far greater than the actual cost of the items involved. So temper your Christmas with the notion of Christmas in, Christmas out. If you are blessed with new things at Christmas, consider what can go out after Christmas, perhaps to bless others. (Another good time for applying the in–out policy is the beginning of the school year.)

One final thought. Be sensitive to the world's poor and the American life of privilege. Excessive or conspicuous consumption is not a positive trait to teach or model to your children.

put it where you can find it

What about the things you don't use very often but that are too valuable or sentimental to throw away or give away, such as memorabilia, family treasures, and thousands of other things? Let me describe a permanent storage system that works well for us. Have you ever searched for something you knew was somewhere in the house but couldn't find, only to find it 10 minutes after buying a duplicate? If so, this storage system is for you.

This system is based on a series of identically sized, sturdy storage boxes. Ideally, these boxes have no printing or writing on them. I began my storage system with 10 heavy duty cardboard boxes (15 x 12 x 10 inches) purchased from a stationery store. The average home needs 12 to 15 to begin. I now have 47 boxes. You can expand the number of boxes as your needs increase: more children, larger house, new hobbies. The boxes are stored together if possible. Mine are on shelves along the wall of my garage.

Pack your boxes with items that relate to each other, then number the front and sides of each box clearly. For example, box 18 at our house contains David's high school and college memorabilia. Before his 20-year high school reunion, he took down box 18 and pulled out his varsity sweater, yearbook, photos of classmates, and programs from school stage presentations to show me. When we got to the reunion, I enjoyed it because I "knew" his friends even though they didn't know me.

I doubt that David will look at box 18 again until his next big reunion. But it will be there when he wants it.

If more than one box holds related materials (such as three boxes of books), you may wish to number them in alphabetical sequence (7-A, 7-B, 7-C). Use a similar sequence for Christmas boxes. No matter how many boxes you need to begin your storage system, number all your Christmas boxes with 25 (25-A, 25-B, 25-C, etc., for December 25) and keep them together.

Once you fill a box, list its contents on a 3 x 5-inch card, one card for each box. In one corner of each card write a memo about where the box is stored (attic, garage, basement, closet at the lake cottage, etc.). In another corner write the number of the box. Keep your packet of index cards in a convenient place where they will be accessible to everyone in the family. If you generate this list on your computer, make sure you have a hard copy handy for family members to refer to easily.

Do you see what you can do? You can go through your entire house, locate and sort things that need to be stored, and actually put them where they are accessible but won't distract you. And it looks good too! How's that for order?

What happens when you want to empty a box? I store my craft projects in my storage system, and sometimes my interest in them is renewed and I actually finish one. For example, I started an afghan that I expected to finish in a month or so. I worked on the afghan for several months, leaving it in a decorative box in our family room. But when I realized I was only working on it about once a month, that was it. I put all the afghan components into a plastic bag and stored them in box 15 in the garage.

Four years went by. I decided that an afghan would be a great Christmas present. So I went to the garage and pulled the half-finished afghan, yarn, needle, and instructions out of box 15. I attacked the project with renewed vigor, and had my Christmas present ready by early December.

So what happened to box 15? Absolutely nothing. The empty box remained on the shelf in the garage, but I tore up the index card. When I needed a new storage box for that year's tax info, I wrote up a new card for box 15.

Here's an additional suggestion for your storage system. Put a red circle or brightly colored star on any of your boxes that contain priceless, irreplaceable family items, such as photographs, special scrapbooks, or old letters. If your house is ever endangered by fire or flood, grab these specially marked boxes on the way out if possible.[2]

Getting your home in order and keeping it that way may sound tiring to you, but it's saving you an even greater fatigue. What really makes you tired? Think about it for a moment. It's not what you do but what you don't do—the things you postpone, not the things you accomplish—that make you tired. If you don't order your household or use a storage system, you will avoid cleaning certain closets or cupboards because they are so messy. The thought of these cluttered areas will continually nag at you. In my home it's the large expanse of Mexican tile that seems to nag at me to be mopped. It's the nagging of things undone that wears you down and makes you tired.

Give yourself a break. Make it a priority to keep your nest in order! And train your children to do the same!

help your children learn to work

When Anissa was young, let me tell you, she wasn't much of an early morning person! When she got out of bed, it took her a long time to get her engine revved and to get going on the tasks that were before her.

On Saturdays, particularly, her dad and I would get up early and roar around the house, working fast and furiously. Anissa would straggle out of her bedroom looking a little disheveled, eyes full of wonder at all the activity. On some of those Saturdays we found that her disposition wasn't as sweet as we hoped it would be. But we discovered that one of the things that improved her disposition was to put her to work.

I'll never forget one Saturday morning when Anissa was 10. We had 10 tons of gravel delivered to our front yard (we live in Arizona, and gravel passes for grass!). The task of the day was to spread the gravel on the yard. David and I were already out shoveling away when Anissa wandered out in her pajamas around nine o'clock in the morning.

She seemed a little grumpy, so we told her to get dressed, eat breakfast, and join us in the yard, which she did—reluctantly. We gave her a small shovel and showed her how to use it to load gravel into the wheelbarrow. She was not a happy camper. She didn't want to work in the yard, and she made her feelings clear by every movement of her body and the few words that slipped from her lips. But with every load of gravel she shoveled, we noticed her disposition improving. After she had worked for an hour or so she was bright and amiable.

This may be an example of what Dr. James Dobson talks about in his book *Hide or Seek*. He contends that you improve a child's self-image and disposition not by saying to them "You look great" or "Your eyes are beautiful," but by recognizing and rewarding them for the tasks they accomplish with their own hands. So, for example, you don't compliment your little girl for her beautiful hair but because she brushed it well. According to Dr. Dobson, how a child sees himself is directly proportionate to what the child accomplishes. Teach your child by word and example that work is good, and that God is the giver of the energy and strength we need to accomplish our tasks. Give your children tasks appropriate to their ages. Here are a few suggestions.

age 2–3:
- Pick up toys
- Put things back where they belong
- Add nonbreakables to table settings
- Brush teeth
- Pull covers off the bed

age 4:
- Set the table
- Help wash dishes or load dishwasher
- Be responsible for feeding and grooming a pet
- Make simple sandwich or cold cereal breakfast
- Help with housework, push vacuum, dust furniture

age 5:
- Help with dinner preparation: tear lettuce, butter bread
- Make bed
- Scour sink
- Make phone calls

age 6:
- Choose clothing
- Keep room in order
- Prepare school lunch
- Tie own shoes
- Gather wood for fireplace
- Help mom or dad with more complicated cleaning jobs

age 7:
- Take phone messages
- Water lawn
- Carry in the groceries

- Do flat ironing (use hankies, napkins, pillowcases so the children can iron them!)
- Clean car inside, help wash outside

age 8:

- Be responsible for personal hygiene
- Complete school assignments
- Sew on a button or mend a tear
- Help with cooking: read recipes, learn cooking instructions
- Help with young children
- Polish silver
- Sweep walkways

age 9–10:

- Do chores without reminders
- Have a pen pal
- Do their own laundry
- Help with the grocery shopping
- Change bed linens
- Clean bedroom and bath (vacuum, dust, scrub tub and toilets)
- Learn more about money management

age 11:

- Earn money: babysitting, mother's helper, yard work
- Learn about banking
- Have a clothing allowance

Here's one final thought about order in the home and the work you do as an at-home mom: A home is to be lived in. It's not a museum. Some order is essential to a healthy, growing, loving family. Absolute order is not.

For example, I met a mom with two small boys. These parents

crave absolute order. They buy no toys for their boys that have small pieces. No trains, trucks, blocks, soldiers, or models are allowed. Too messy. A few big stuffed animals are available for them.

Perhaps these parents are taking order to an unrealistic extreme. Wouldn't it be better to have a small room or area where the boys could play with "messy," creative, stimulating toys of all sizes? Anissa took a corner of her family room and tacked up a world map. She put her son's toys in the nook, and at 6 months he was drawn to the area as his own play place. Even a mess can be controlled if you designate a place for it. That's order, too!

making money at home

A Bil Keane comic strip, Family Circus, shows in three scenes, a wife reading the paper, a wife asking her husband, "Would you like to work at home?" And the husband thinks for a minute, conjures up all the "home" activities (TV, children running, playing, crying, eating, the dogs and cats running around and says firmly, "No way!" Yet the Bureau of Labor and Statistics reported that in May 2004, 20.7 million persons did some work at home as part of their primary job.

"I want to stay at home, but economically I can't do it."

"If I could afford it, I would rather be at home with my children."

Everywhere I go I hear remarks like these from tearful moms who genuinely want to be at home. For these women, working outside the home interferes with their full-time job of being a wife and mother. Yet they have to earn money or some sort of resources. Some say outside employment is simply an economic fact of life for most women in today's expensive, modern world. And, yes, it is difficult to stay at home without any income. We all have financial obligations to meet and debts to pay. And some factors are predetermined—especially taxes.

Second incomes seem like a large financial boon to most families, but according to Parents Magazine, many couples discover they are clearing only 10 to 20 percent of that second paycheck. Financial experts say the average family can cut 20 percent from their current expenses without feeling the pinch. So if you are determined to make full-time parenting a reality, chances are you can do it more easily than you think. You need to attack the big-ticket expense items like credit cards, insurance policy deductibles, car costs, utilities, and vacations. In every case, through careful shopping, you can save money.

The cost of child-rearing contiues to grow. Today's cost is nearing the $200,000 mark! But being an at-home mom can be done! You can still make ends meet. Lots of moms are doing it by making some money at home. You just need conviction, discipline, and a plan.

Conviction. You must be personally convinced in word and deed that family is a top priority. Your family must share your conviction. If your children are very small, you may have to stick with your conviction for 10 to 15 more years. If your kids are adolescents, your commitment is shorter. But whatever your situation, you must believe that staying at home is right for you.

Discipline. I believe a primary reason moms work is to get the family out of debt. I am aware of high taxes and the growing cost of living. Discipline yourself to get out of debt so the family financial burden becomes manageable. Get out of debt so you won't need as much money to sustain your family. Get out of debt so you don't need to work at all.

Discipline yourself to constantly project what you need monthly to get out of debt (not so you can buy something else!). Carefully survey your expenses, income, and how much you'll have left to live on. Measure how long it will be until you can concentrate full-time on raising your children and meeting all your needs on one income.

A plan. For some women, the conviction to work at home and the discipline to get out of debt will mean enormous changes in their lifestyles. Whatever your circumstance, set a plan for freedom from debt and begin to work toward it. You may have to work at home for a number of years to reach your goal. Or you may be able to retire your debt and begin living on one income in a short time.

For a single mom who faces a long-term commitment to a job,

your goal may be to maximize your time at home by minimizing your expenses. Or consider other options that are becoming more acceptable, such as flex time, a compressed work week, telecommuting, job sharing, or voluntary reduced time.

Sometimes your goal may lead you to sell the large home you hold near and dear. Can you sacrifice your dream home to stay at home with your children? Your goal is freedom. Don't lose sight of that.

women in the workforce

When I was a young girl my father owned a dry-cleaning business. The store was in the front of the building, and our apartment—a small bedroom, living room, and kitchen—was in the back. That's where our family lived and worked together.

There aren't many family-owned-and-operated, live-in businesses like ours anymore. It was common practice for many centuries, even back to ancient times, for men and women to work together at home earning a living and raising the children. Most families lived where they worked and worked where they lived, especially when America's work was primarily farming.

But the Industrial Revolution of the nineteenth century removed many men, women, and children from their farms and brought them into the cities to run the factories. This change had an enormous impact on the family unit and childcare.

Around the turn of the century, there was concern about women and children working in the factories. A very successful labor leader, Samuel Gompers, fought for giving men "a living wage" large enough to support a family. Not much later, Henry Ford called for "a family wage," which he said was necessary to "avoid the hideous prospect of little children and their mothers being forced out to work."

During Franklin D. Roosevelt's presidency, another voice was raised in favor of freeing women from having to work even at home. Mary Anderson, a New Deal reformer and critic of the U.S. Labor Department, said, "The only thing to do about home work is to abolish it and to arrange for higher wages for the breadwinner in a family so that the wife and children do not have to supplement the family income by doing home work."[1]

This concept was readily accepted until the early 1960s. Since then, women have been going back to work inside and outside the home for many reasons. Some women work because the family needs the money for basic living expenses. Others work because labor-saving devices in the home have freed them to enter the workforce in hopes of raising the family's standard of living. For still others, the feminist movement played a role in their decision to go back to work to make a statement of a woman's worth in the workforce.

As I travel and talk to women, I hear about many husbands who approach their employers to say, "I need a raise. My family is growing, and our needs have changed." Often the employer responds, "Well, your wife can get a job." It seems that sending a wife out to work is easier than raising a man's wages today. I certainly appreciate people like Samuel Gompers, Henry Ford, and Mary Anderson, who value moms at home.

There were 64.7 million employed women in the U.S. in 2004, about 46 percent of the total labor force, down from 47 percent in 2003. According to the Department of Labor, 74 percent of those women worked full-time and the remaining 26 percent worked part-time. Approximately 4 million women were self-employed in nonagricultural industries. Labor force participation rates for women, by race, were: black, 61.5 percent; white, 58.9 percent; Asian, 57.6 percent; and Hispanic, 56.1 percent. Only Hispanic women increased the percentage of participation in the labor force from 2003 to 2004.

Fortune magazine recently reported that now more than ever employers are willing to consider unconventional work arrangements—job sharing, telecommuting, and part-time positions—to attract and retain workers. So women have more room to negotiate. Technology also makes it easier for women to work from home. Working for a New York firm and living in Nebraska is now possible.

working at home

The turn of the twenty-first century brought an even more significant change into the family unit. Technology, while not new, has made positive inroads to help a family balance the budget and work together as a unit. In many ways the advance technology and the increased availability are letting families own and operate their own businesses from home akin to the agrarian culture of the nineteenth century.

The Center for Research on Information Technology and Organizations studied actual home environments to determine how personal computers and the Internet are currently being used in the home, how life in the home is being impacted by these information technologies, and the attitudes and potential interest that family members have about new technologies that will be on the market in the next several years. They found some interesting things. For example, the use of rooms has changed due to computers, but the structural space was generally not modified to accommodate these changes. We simply added furniture and adjusted our internal space in the home. Women and children were identified as important "change agents" for technology (those who introduced new information technology into the home). One problem identified was the fact that a PC is a single user product, which separates parents and children. New evolving technology may permit multiple users to "interface," as the techies say, with each other.

I met Kim and her husband when I first moved to Arizona. I loved to visit them in their home, partly because it was so lovely and well-decorated.

Several years ago, Kim and her husband moved to Chicago. They bought a bigger, lovelier house. Kim decided that she needed to go to work to help pay for the house, the extras, and the expenses of moving from Arizona to Illinois.

She got a job that required her to leave home before dawn, and she didn't return until after dark. Week after week this went on. Soon she realized she was spending all week working to keep a house she could only enjoy on weekends. She told me that during the winter she spent only 13 hours of daylight a week in her home. Kim realized that working outside the home was not helping her achieve her family goals. She was very eager at that point to make a change.

For many women, working outside the home isn't financially worth the effort. Consider the tax rate alone for just a minute. If a married couple brings in more than $59,400, the tax rate is 15 percent. And if their income is more than $119,950, the rate is a whopping 25 percent. And, basically, more than 80 cents of every dollar earned by the average working woman goes to childcare, meals at work, gas, and clothing. This leaves 20 cents or less, per dollar, in disposable income to pay for eating out, entertainment, household help she may need, laundry and dry cleaning, and other incidentals. Not much left, is there?

Working at home is one way to gain the benefits of increased family income for expenses and debt reduction without seriously disrupting the family. What does working at home look like? Home-based employment, or cottage industries, is more widespread than you may think. Several major companies, including Honeywell, Aetna, JC Penney, American Express, AT&T, and Blue Cross/Blue Shield, use home-based telecommunications for word processing, telemarketing, and other clerical functions, opening up numerous opportunities for women working at home. In 2002, the Bureau of Labor Statistics reported nearly 7 million Americans were self-employed persons with home-based businesses. Half of those were in management, professional, and related occupations. About a fifth were in sales from home.

One *Wall Street Journal* headline reported "Stay-at-home moms get entrepreneurial." The featured woman in the article was Tamara Monosoff, a former business consultant and Clinton White House staffer, who quit work to stay at home when her daughter was born. The mom found she got annoyed when her child continuously unrolled the toilet paper. So she invented a special latch to prevent the problem, which sells for $6.95 to parents and pet owners. She projected sales in 2005 of more than $1 million. Tamara authored the book *The Mom Inventor's Handbook: How to Turn Your Great Idea into the Next Big Thing*. Another mom invented and marketed a nonspill snack cup.

Julie Aigner-Clark created innovative baby videos and other products that encouraged interaction between infants and adults. Called Baby Einstein, the company quickly grew and was bought out by the Walt Disney Company in 2001. Schoolteacher Victoria Knight-McDowell worked with health professionals to develop a dietary supplement called Air-Borne that allegedly prevents or counters cold symptoms. You too can allow your one-of-a-kind brain power to go for it. Be unique and uncommon, embracing God's imprint on your life.

There is one caution, however. When you ask what type of work you should take on, remember your top priority—your family. If your main reason for working at home is to get out of debt so you can live contentedly and sufficiently on one income, beware of seeking a job primarily because of the great personal stimulation, satisfaction, or gratification it brings you. Why? Because you may get so interested and involved in growing your business, finding new customers, and making more money that you lose sight of your goal—like Sally did. She started a muffin-baking business in her home, and it prospered. But soon she was baking 2,000 muffins a week—and her goal for being at home was lost.

Rather, choose a job within your circle of general interest that helps you accomplish your goal as soon as possible. Work until you pay off your debts, then limit the hours you put into your business (based on the needs of your family) or close the door on that job and move on to full-time mothering.

getting down to business

Have a plan. When I was first asked to speak publicly, a friend suggested I get an agent. I thought about my plan and how long it would take before I could take speaking engagements more than a few times a month. My husband and I decided that we would take the traversing-down-the-mountain approach versus the snowplow approach. An agent would have begun booking me (advertising me), but I wanted to take it slowly. We never hired an agent, and the word-of-mouth approach has certainly worked. I have more invitations than I can accept.

When planning a home business, there are several questions you need to answer in order to understand the legal, financial, logistical, and scheduling ramifications of your business.

General. If you are a product or service business, consider: Who are your customers? Do you have some currently? If not, where will you find customers? Are your sales done in your home? Or someplace else? Where? If you have to deliver your products, how will it affect your car? What is your advertising plan? Is it word of mouth, referral, or actual advertisements?

Legal. Are there any city, county, state, or federal restrictions, deed restrictions, or local zoning requirements that prohibit you from conducting business in your neighborhood? Do you need a business license for what you plan to do?

Financial. Perhaps you need to draw up a budget and consider in advance the financial impact of your new business. What will it cost to start this business? What kind of capital will you need to invest? What taxes will you incur, and how will you pay them? Do you have some kind of bookkeeping system for filing invoices, reports, and tax forms? Do you need equipment? Do you need inventory? Where will you store the inventory? If you have a mail-order business, where will you mail the products from? What about capital?

In her book *101 Ways to Make Money at Home,* Gwen Ellis offers business ideas and includes the amount of capital needed to start each business.

Logistical. How will you keep your work from interrupting your family life? Do you need another telephone line, an office, or special work area? Will your work take over a full room in the house, half a room, or a closet? Do you need special supplies for this job and, if so, where will these supplies be stored? Will you have employees? Part-time or full-time? What about insurance? Can you keep books?

Scheduling. How will you schedule your work around your mothering responsibilities? Is it possible to do your work in just a few hours in the afternoon while your children are napping or will you need six hours a day? Maybe you will have to get up in the morning before the children are up and put in an hour of work, then work during their naps and again in the evening after they have gone to bed.

The following resources, some Christian and some secular, will help you answer some of these important questions as you consider your business.

- The Small Business Administration will give you as much information as you need to start a home-based business. Check out www.sba.com. Start here so you don't face the lack of information once you are immersed in your new work at home.
- Mothers Home Business Network, P.O. Box 423, East Meadow, NY 11554, (516) 997-7394. Also check out www.homework ingmom.com.
- Internal Revenue Service Publication 587, "Business Use of Your Home."

Stumped for what kind of work to do? Here's a list of money-making businesses for at-home moms (and their kids):

service-oriented businesses

Babysitting	Computer services
Drop-off babysitting	Editing/proofreading
Desktop publishing	Resumé writing
Elderly respite care	Typing
Pet grooming	Mailing lists
Pet-sitting	Envelope stuffing
Housesitting	Telephone answering
Housecleaning	Apartment management

Tax preparation
Bookkeeping/accounting
Catering
Flower and balloon delivery
Party planning
Vacation planning
Online instruction
Teaching classes
  (exercise, art)
Seasonal work such as
  Christmas wrapping
Sewing/alterations/
  upholstery

Newspaper delivery
Nail and hair care
Ironing
Residential Care at Home
Adjunct professor
Bed & Breakfast
Home organization
Babysitting for Bible studies
  and support groups
Gardening/lawn service/
  plant care
Christmas home decorating

product-oriented businesses
(make, sell, repair)

Candles
Dolls and doll clothing
Framed and unframed art
Stained glass
Gift baskets
Photography
Cooking and baking
Telephone sales
Cosmetics
Kitchen supplies
Calligraphy
  (announcements, etc.)

Ceramics
Flower arranging
Jewelry
Furniture
Toys
Other arts and crafts
Cake decorating
Mail order
Home decorating
Art—any medium

Let me comment about a couple of these business opportunities.

Consider newspaper delivery. What a great idea! I know a number of women who have found it to be a very fruitful source of income. An early morning paper route of 100 to 200 homes can net you $300 to $600 per month. You need a car, of course, and you will put some miles on it. You can even share a route with a friend. It would be great fun driving around in the quiet hours of the morning together, throwing papers and steadily climbing out of debt. And you can cover for each other when a child is ill or during vacations.

Many newspaper moms have told me that they were amazed how God rewarded their determination to be debt-free at-home moms. He gave them rest in spirit and body that they normally wouldn't have felt because of rising so early.

Help other women organize their closets, kitchens, etc. My daughter founded a business called Woman Friday based on this very concept.

Food preparation on a small scale is an excellent way to provide good meals for your family while serving a working mom. There are some working moms in your community who would pay you well to prepare sack lunches for their children or cook evening meals they can pick up on the way home from work. As one mom said, "When you're already cooking for four, it's not much more trouble to cook for eight."

Can it really happen for you? Deedee discovered that it can. Deedee is a single mom I heard about who received some child support but not enough to meet her family's needs. Deedee was determined to do what she could to get out of debt without taking a regular outside job.

First she moved from an expensive-to-live-in large city to a small community. In the exchange she dropped her house payment considerably. She earns money in many creative ways. She delivers telephone directories once a year. She has also delivered newspapers and sold Avon. When the priests in her parish needed someone to cook and clean, Deedee earned money by shopping for groceries, preparing meals at home and delivering them, and cleaning the rectory. If this single, at-home mom can reach her goal through conviction and discipline, so can you.

The idea of earning money at home to defer expenses and get out of debt is fairly common. Let me add one more idea, as we close this topic. Consider as a family unit a way to earn money for special projects in your community, church, city, or state. Perhaps your church could give you some suggestions. Read the newspaper and pray for God to give you ideas that will work for you and your situation.

saving money at home

Don't do without. Just do it for less.

Nearly 10 years ago I was standing in a line and looked down at the exact moment a young man looked down and we simultaneously spotted a copper penny on the floor. As the older woman, I nodded to him, suggesting he could have the penny. He vigorously declined and I bent to pick up the penny, dropping it into a wee pouch I carry in my purse.

One penny. Can one penny matter? *Yes!* For 18 years I saved every penny that crossed my path for the purchase of my daughter's wedding dress. The story spread and several faithful friends contributed handfuls of pennies from time to time. My daughter's wedding program read, "We thank the several faithful friends who over the past 18 years donated pennies toward the cost of Anissa's wedding dress. It is paid in full, one penny at a time. The first penny is sown in the hem of her gown." In fact our pennies paid for her shoes, veil, and headpiece.

every penny matters!

For years I have been called thrifty, careful, frugal, and, yes, even cheap! I am glad to be associated with being a good steward of all I have been given.

My motto is never to buy "cheap" stuff, but always buy as cheaply as I can. Cheap items are usually inferior quality goods. I never settle for that kind of product. As a woman, wife, and mother, you're probably the major purchaser in your family. That means you must know goods and merchandise well. Don't be duped by the lower price when you are getting less or lower quality.

To be honest, I don't like to shop, but I love to "make a deal." Actually, I love the thrill of the kill in making a deal. My husband has assigned the negotiating in auto purchases to me. We do the research, look for a used car, estimate the value, and offer what is reasonable, never trying to undermine the seller. Then I go to work in the give and take of making the deal.

Another cost-saving tactic is wardrobe. I wear only black and white clothes, which allows me to seldom need anything basic. I just continue to augment my existing wardrobe. When you live this kind of lifestyle you find yourself in good economic company: Bill Gates still flying in coach; Rick Warren giving 90 percent of his income away; Warren Buffet still living in his first home purchased over 40 years ago for about $30,000. Even John Adams, our nation's second president, praised thriftiness. He wrote to his wife, "Let frugality and industry be our virtues." Her reply, "I endeavor to live in the most frugal manner possible."

Parents magazine, in 2000, indicated that families can cut 20 percent off their spending without feeling the pinch. The difference in stretching dollars and cutting costs may assist you in making being a full-time mom at-home a reality.

Being content with where you are and what you have is the key to surviving a frugal lifestyle in order to reach your goal of being an at-home mom.

33 great ways to stretch your dollars

The best way to save money at home is to make everything you own last as long as possible. The next thing is to spend less on the goods and services you buy. Here are practical ideas for getting the most out of your dollar.

1. *Maintain your appliances.* Defrost your freezer regularly; it will last longer. Vacuum the coils on the back of the refrigerator. Remove lint promptly from the lint filter in your dryer. Service large appliances regularly, including air conditioner/heating systems, pools, sound systems, and garbage disposals.

2. *Maintain your automobile.* The average American family buys seven new cars in a lifetime and spends upwards of $120,000 on interest. Save money by buying clean, used cars in good condition for cash instead of financing new cars. Make a monthly payment to yourself instead of to the finance company or the bank. This becomes a savings account for buying your next car with cash.

Keep your cars longer than a year or two. Keep them until they have 100,000 miles on them. We have found it best to secure an all-around mechanic who can care for all our car's needs instead of taking it to costly specialists.

Own just one car. The savings can be significant even if you own your car free and clear. Watch God provide means of transportation.

3. *Don't over-wash clothes and linens.* For example, if a tablecloth has only one spot on it, it doesn't need to go into the washer. It just needs a spot cleaning. Do your husband's shirts at home instead of having them laundered. Don't dry clean your clothes too often, and don't dry clean everything. Wools and most other fabrics can be gentle-washed in the machine or hand-washed. Also, hanging your clothes on 10-cent plastic hangers will make them last longer than hanging them on wire hangers. Always hang up your clothes as soon as you take them off.

4. *Practice "trading off" or "bartering" for some of your services.* Have a doctor or dentist or hair stylist do some work for your family while you provide what you are best at. This will allow you to accomplish the same tasks without the need for cash.

5. *Food management is a huge way to save money.* Use coupons at the grocery store. The Manufacturer's Coupon Control Center reports that shoppers who use an average number of coupons—five to eight per trip—cut $6.31 from their bill each week. The annual savings adds up to $328. If you use nine or more coupons per week, your total annual savings could exceed $500. Also, buy foods in bulk whenever possible. (See idea 12.)

Using coupons is not corny—it saves costs. So serious is the subject that September is designated "National Coupon Month." Promotion Marketing Association reports in the year 2000 more than 75 percent of homes in America saved over $800, with a national savings of 6 billon dollars. Interestingly, the income range of coupon cutters is $50,000 to $75,000. Also, the higher the level of education, the more people are prone to snipping a coupon. It makes sense to be smart people. Be one.

6. *Participate in food sharing.* Food-sharing programs are springing up all over the United States. David and I were part of one in the southwest region. We paid a small fee and donated two hours of volunteer service monthly (church work, babysitting for others count). In return we received four times our fee in top-grade foods, including meats, vegetables, rice or pasta, and fresh fruit. Look for a food-sharing program in your area.

7. *Use generic brands.* Products with local store brands and generic brands are usually cheaper than the major national brands with the same quality. Use dishwashing liquid instead of the expensive brand-name products for hand-washing delicate fabrics. Avoid "end-cap" products...those expensive items located at the end of store shelves.

Buy chicken by the pound, not by the brand name. Look for plumpness in the chicken.

Ask your doctor and pharmacist for generic drugs if they're available.

Order your checks from a mail-order house, such as Checks Unlimited, instead of from your bank. The charges are much less.

8. *Don't forget menu planning.* It's the most money-saving activity a family can do. Plan all seven days of three meals per day if possible. If you can't do that, at least plan breakfasts and dinners. Be sure you use a market list as you plan your meals.

Plan menus weekly. Research shows that you save 30 percent more than the gal who does not menu plan. Never go to the market without a list, and buy only what's on your list—nothing more, nothing less. Spend only 30 minutes in the market on each trip. Research indicates that you spend $2.50 every minute you're in the store after the first 30. Think about it. With lists and menus most of us can get in and out of the store in 30 minutes, not counting the time you spend chatting with your neighbor.

9. *Recycle, reuse, refurbish.* I've been thrifty and ecologically minded for a long time–especially when it comes to paper products. I don't buy paper plates or napkins, and I'm very judicious about how I use paper towels. I use old clothes and rags to do my home-cleaning instead of expensive, disposable cleaning towels. I use finger towels for napkins. Not only is it cheaper, but it saves a lot of frustration at the table when the little ones spill something. I can pick up the mess very easily with a little towel I'm already using as a napkin. The towels are laundered and reused repeatedly.

We live in a throwaway society, but it's expensive and unwise. If you want to save money, be cautious about throwing something away that can be reused. For example, wash and reuse your Ziploc bags. Recycle cans and bottles. And consider using cloth diapers instead of throwaways. Research has proven that even paying for a cloth-diaper laundering service is less expensive than using throwaway diapers. Convenience is usually synonymous with greater cost.

Avoid as many disposable products as possible. For example, you can save about $20 per year by using a standard razor with longer lasting replacement blades instead of disposable razors.

10. *Pay high deductibles and lower premiums.* It is estimated that you can save 15 to 40 percent on your annual premiums for auto and

home insurance by raising your deductible. Call your insurance agent to find out exactly how much you can save. And don't forget that equipping your house with smoke detectors will save you at least 2 percent on your insurance premium. Regularly review insurance plans and coverage. Reconsider your deductibles as your incomes fluctuate. Include, vision, dental, homeowners, renter's policies, automobile, etc.

11. *Watch your spending.* When you go shopping, carry only the cash you need. Leave your credit cards at home, and stay away from cash machines.

Don't shop at convenience stores; they're more expensive. Go to supermarkets or large stores. The last time I looked, a package of two flashlight batteries was $3.59 at the convenience store and $2.89 at the supermarket—a difference of 70 cents. A quart of milk at the convenience store averaged 12 cents more than at the supermarket. And a dozen eggs was 66 cents cheaper at the supermarket. Also, don't buy drug-store items in the market. They usually cost 15 to 25 percent more.

12. *Buy economy sizes and repackage them at home.* Consider repackaging foods like chips. I love Cheetos. (I know, I know, they do not belong in the four basic food groups.) Maybe your kids do too. Buy one large bag instead of the individual packets and repackage them at home in small Ziploc bags for their lunches. And save the Ziplocs for reuse. Shop at janitorial supply shops for cleaning agents in your home. They will sell you larger quantities. They also will help you select proper cleaning agents for your home and teach you how to use less.

13. *Reduce costs on magazines and newspapers.* Subscribe to magazines and periodicals you have been buying monthly at the newsstand. You'll pay about half the cover price when you subscribe. You may even want to share a subscription with another family.

If you receive the newspaper every day but don't read the daily edition, subscribe only to the Sunday edition. If you don't read the Sunday paper, subscribe only to the daily paper.

14. *Be careful about eating out.* Check out how much money you spend eating lunches out, even if it's only at fast-food places. You'll be surprised. If you're "doing lunch" with a friend, consider packing a lunch and eating at the park instead of spending money to eat out. Also send home-packed lunches with your husband and children whenever possible.

For 30 years, David took a packed-at-home lunch consisting of one egg, yogurt, a green apple, and a few carrots. The average daily cost? $1.20. If lunch out averaged $5 daily, he saved $34,500 in lunch cost alone!

And how about those snacks when you're out for the evening? It may be just an ice cream cone or frozen yogurt after church or popcorn and drinks at the movies, but they add up. Also, don't forget that early-bird dinners and movies are often less expensive before six in the evening. Figure out what you are spending and cut back where you can. Remember: The money you save is the same as money earned to reduce your debt and help you reach your stay-at-home goal. And you don't have to pay income tax on it!

15. *Join a babysitting co-op or trade with another family on a regular basis.* Be sure to establish guidelines before you begin this way of life. It will save you the dilemma of misunderstandings regarding how many hours per month each family will use, when, what time of day, etc.

16. *Shop at garage sales,* especially for children's toys and clothing. Be careful not to buy more than you need just because "it's so cheap."

17. *Sell your used belongings at garage sales or consignment stores.* Consider trading clothes with a friend. I used to share clothes with a friend who lived in my town, but traveled in different social circles.

18. *Color coordinate wardrobes for yourself and your children.* You

may not want to go to my extreme (I wear primarily black and white clothes), but a basic color scheme will save time and money.

19. *Hang clothes on the line or an in-house rack.* It saves the dryer from running, and reduces wear and tear on the garments.

20. *Buy used books.*

21. *Consider heating costs.* Can you use wood? Gas? Something less expensive than what you currently use? When our electric dryer died of old age, I purchased a gas dryer. In the 10 years we have used the gas dryer (it's still going) we expected to save $256 per year in energy bills. Check all appliances for energy ratings before you purchase them. In 2006, natural gas has had a 40 percent increase. Compare energy costs before you choose.

22. *Make holidays and special days creatively inexpensive.* Make a game of this. What can we do for under $10? We still do this, not because we need to, but because it is genuinely more beneficial to spend time thinking and planning an event carefully, than just heading for the most expensive restaurant. (Although it is fun to have a fine meal from time to time in a lovely restaurant.)

23. *DVDs and popcorn at home are still among our favorites.*

24. *Can you trim, or even cut, a family member's hair?* Try it. My David is very bald now, but I have cut his hair ever since we were married (even when he had some).

25. *Plant a few vegetable plants.* If you have a yard, try a garden. If not, a pot of tomatoes or zucchini will save money and provide an education for the children.

26. *Revitalize leather products.* Anissa had a favorite black leather belt. She wore it nearly every day. The edges of the belt looked worn and dull. She wanted a new one (I agreed that the belt looked forlorn), but I took it to a shoemaker who redyed and polished the leather, making it look brand-new for $3.50. A shoemaker will resew

purses and belts, as well as redye shoes, belts, and purses at very little cost. Consider it.

27. *Have a budget.* Prepare it in writing and live by it. If you have problems sticking to a budget, check out Consumer Credit Counseling Services, which is a national nonprofit agency. They will assist you by providing free service for preparing a written budget for your family. Read any of Larry Burkett's materials on financial planning.

28. *Consider buying and selling on eBay.* If you have a computer, do this yourself...or offer the job to your children.

29. *Stretching your family dollars* might include your children earning money to offset their wants and needs. Children can babysit, dog sit, be mother's helpers; teens can run errands, do housecleaning, baking, and cooking for others to name a few tasks.

30. *When buying furniture consider the pieces you are selecting being used in any room of the house.* Except for beds and appliances I never buy a piece of furniture that I cannot move into any room in our home.

31. *Watch overdue fees!* "Early is on-time" is another Otto motto that saves money. Know your credit cycles and due dates to avoid late charges.

32. *Keep accurate spending records and review regularly.*

33. *Share in as many ways as you can think of.* Annie J. and I purchased a freezer together before we could afford to purchase our own. (As an added bonus, I got to see her more often.)

be content

The apostle Paul said he learned to be content in whatever financial state he was in, whether in abundance or want (see Philippians 4:11-12). Being content with where you are and what you have is the key to surviving a frugal lifestyle in order to reach your goal of being an at-home mom.

Over 25 years ago, David and I moved into the house we're living in now. The living room and dining room were carpeted with a rather low-quality celery-green carpet. Celery green doesn't go very well with most of our furnishings. But we knew this was the house the Lord wanted for us, so we had to deal with the carpet.

It would have been nice to buy new carpet, but it wasn't in the budget. So I immediately called the carpet-man and found that I could have the carpet dyed for about $200. We'd dyed carpets before, so I knew it would stretch the life of the carpet. So we dyed our celery-green carpet charcoal gray.

Seven years later our gray carpet was sun-streaked and faded. There were dark spots where the furniture had been sitting. The living room had survived one flood (in Arizona!), and the water-damaged carpet was literally falling apart.

We looked at our budget and decided there was no way we could afford to buy a new carpet. I was disappointed because the room was a bit of an embarrassment. Yet I was absolutely determined to trust God for my carpeting and be content with what I had. It wasn't easy.

As wives, we put ourselves in a very precarious place. We want so many things, and when we're home all day we tend to see the things we want even more clearly. We are quick to think how nice it would be to have a little piece of fabric for this room or a new chair or a bedspread in the master bedroom. It's easy to become discontent. I had some of those feelings about my carpet. But I earnestly asked the Lord to give me a heart of contentment and gratitude for the many things He had given me and to help me wait patiently for the opportunity to purchase a new carpet.

My prayer was answered in a most unusual way. After I had prayed about my carpet for almost 18 months, two decorator friends came to me and asked if they could help me spruce up the house a little by rearranging some of the furniture and moving some wall decorations around. I was delighted. Soon they began moving things around—and not just one or two pieces.

Our family room became the dining room, and the dining room is now a library. A sofa was moved from the living room to the master bedroom. Overall, a wonderful new look came over our house without my spending a dime. I was most grateful for this gracious gift.

At the same time this was going on, a dear sister in our church family was moving into another home, which happened to be much larger than ours. My decorator friends discovered that she was going to replace the carpet in her new home, a carpet that was in wonderful condition except for a few slight stains.

You guessed it. God in His providence allowed this dear sister to give us her used carpet. I discovered the carpet's color the day it was installed: white—perfect, of course! I was most grateful for God's provision of that carpet.

Something else wonderful happened. Kim was a young woman who was living with us for a year as our guest in order to get her finances in order before getting her own place. The last month she lived with us was the month the carpet was installed. She not only saw the answer to my prayer unfold, she was part of it. Her financial counselor told her to make a one-month rental payment to us before she moved into her new apartment complex to help her adjust to her new expenses. The money she gave us paid for the installation of our free carpet and covered most of the cost of cleaning it. Our out-of-pocket expense for the carpet was $15. It took nine years to get our carpet, but God is faithful.

Be patient and content. Ask the Lord to help you find a clever way to do the things you want to do in your home without going out and buying everything new.

mentors for mothers

Seek a woman of wisdom as a mentor.

At 28 years old, I had an excellent idea! I was going to find an older woman to be my mentor, to teach me things about life. I was eager to learn. I had a very clear picture of what she would be like. She would be well-groomed, of course (I expected that of anyone who could teach me something). She would be bright and fairly well-educated (at least have a college degree). And she would be a wife and mother who was very active in her community and church.

So I set out to find this woman. But God provided a mentor far beyond my expectations. He gave me a woman of wisdom. In His providence God sent Martha. Martha was raised in the back hills of Arkansas and completed a high-school education. She had a modest home, a husband, and five daughters.

Martha was one of the wealthiest women I have ever known in every important area of life. She had allowed herself to be prepared by the Father to be my mentor. She was ready to be the scriptural older woman in my life (see Titus 2:3-5). She volunteered for the job, and I knew she was serious about investing in me.

Over the next five years (and all the years since), here is what Martha lovingly provided for me:

- marriage advice
- encouragement to firmly discipline my daughter
- guidance on how to survive on a modest income
- advice on how to keep calamities in perspective (calamities happen in a younger mom's life, don't they?)
- a place to weep and rejoice
- and most of all, a truly caring heart

God has a special gift for you as a younger mother: the care and counsel of an older woman. Seek a woman of wisdom as a mentor. The payoff for both of you will be enormous. Are you interested in having a Martha or perhaps being a Martha someday? It's within your grasp. Reach for it.

mentoring: a tested and honorable activity

The original Mentor was a character in Homer's ancient Greek epic poem, the *Odyssey*. Mentor was the man Odysseus entrusted to manage his household and teach his son as he set sail to conquer Troy. Mentor was Odysseus' wise and trusted friend and counselor. His name has become a synonym for any person, usually older, who teaches or coaches another.

Mentoring as an educational process is one of the oldest forms of teaching. Apprenticeship is a type of mentoring. Other words that describe a mentor are life-shaper, guide, role model, nurturer, beacon, and facilitator. Here are several more thoughts to help you understand what a mentor is and does:

- Daniel Levenson describes a mentor as an older man helping a younger man learn the ropes of the working world.[1]
- Ted Engstrom defines mentoring as passing on to someone close, trusted, and experienced what God has given you.[2]

- Fred Smith, a Christian businessman and speaker, says, "A mentor is not a person who can do the work better than his followers; he is a person who can get his followers to do the work better than he can."

- John C. Crosby, of the Uncommon Individual Foundation, says, "Mentoring is a brain to pick, a shoulder to cry on, and a kick in the pants." Crosby also describes this ministry in what he calls, "The Ten Commandments of Mentoring":

  1. Thou shalt not play God.
  2. Thou shalt not play Teacher.
  3. Thou shalt not play Mother or Father.
  4. Thou shalt not lie with your body.
  5. Active listening is the holy time and thou shalt practice it at every session.
  6. Thou shalt be nonjudgmental.
  7. Thou shalt not lose heart because of repeated disappointments.
  8. Thou shalt practice empathy, not sympathy.
  9. Thou shalt not believe that thou can move mountains.
  10. Thou shalt not envy thy neighbor's protégé, nor thy neighbor's success.[3]

Mentoring is also suggested in Scripture as a spiritual ministry:

Like apples of gold in settings of silver is a word spoken in right circumstances. Like an earring of gold and an ornament of fine gold is a wise reprover to a listening ear (Proverbs 25:11-12).

Iron sharpens iron, so one man sharpens another (Proverbs 27:17).

The things which you have heard from me in the presence of many witnesses, these entrust to faithful men, who will be able to teach others also (2 Timothy 2:2).

Older women likewise are to be reverent in their behavior, not malicious gossips, nor enslaved to much wine, teaching what is good, that they may encourage the young women to love their husbands, to love their children, to be sensible, pure, workers at home, kind, being subject to their own husbands, that the word of God may not be dishonored (Titus 2:3-5).

What's the difference between mentoring and discipling? As I see it, discipling is the formal teaching of the Bible, prayer, and other spiritual disciplines. Mentoring, however, involves the "catch it" concept. Mentoring is an informal transfer of life experience from a mentor to a "mentee." A discipler conveys her knowledge; a mentor listens and shares her experiences. Discipling happens best in a classroom or study situation; mentoring happens very nicely over a cup of coffee or a piece of pie. Certainly there is room for both in any relationship, but clearly the focus for a mentor is informal process.

what does a mentor do?

Your chosen mentor should be available for some or all of the following ministries in your life as a younger mom:

1. *Spend time with you and your children.* By spending time with you, your mentor will get to know you and your children. As you get better acquainted, your fellowship, planning, activities, and dialogue together will occur more naturally and without strict scheduling.

2. *Provide counsel.* As she gets to know you and your family, your mentor will be able to counsel you wisely about practical things such as homemaking skills, child discipline, and keeping a balanced spiritual life. The power of a mentor is in her experience and her perspective. The mentor has already made the journey and is a symbol of hope to help younger moms realize, "Maybe I can do it too." Remember, counsel is someone else's advice, not a mandate.

3. *Provide spiritual leadership.* A spiritual leader is a person who influences another person toward God. There are indeed specialized leadership gifts, but spiritual leadership cannot be confined

to these. Consider the apostle Paul's remarks in Philippians 2:3-4. Spiritual leadership begins with a person who is genuinely concerned about the interests of others, who regards others as more important than herself.

4. *Provide support.* What does support look like in a mentor? It includes listening, providing structure, expressing positive expectations, serving as an advocate, sharing herself, and making your time together meaningful.

5. *Provide challenge.* What does challenge look like? It is setting tasks, engaging in discussion, heating up dichotomies, constructing hypotheses, and setting high standards. Effective mentoring requires the right mix of support and challenge.

6. *Provide vision.* How does a mentor provide vision? By offering herself as a model of the kind of mom younger women want to be. Vision means providing a road map to motherhood, suggesting a new language, and providing a mirror to stimulate the younger mom to become whom she wants to be.

7. *Evaluate the process.* At certain places along the way in a mentoring relationship, your mentor should stop and help you take a look at the progress you're making. If the progress is good and the resources are adequate, you may both agree that this is a comfortable, supportive process. If obstacles have appeared, your mentor may be able to help you overcome them or work around them. If obstacles cannot be transcended, you may agree to move back a stage or two and reassess your goals and resources.

how do i find a mentor?

As an at-home mom, you need a mentor. You need to be relating to a woman who has already been down the road you are traveling. You need to be sharing your joys and struggles with her and tapping into the wisdom of her experience.

But where do you find such a person? After all, there isn't a section for mentors in the yellow pages like there is for hairdressers and plumbers.

To find a mentor you need to get to know some mature Christian women. A good place to start is in your church or women's Bible-study group. But don't restrict your search to the women up front—the pastor's wife, the Bible-study leader, the women's ministries coordinator. If you look closely enough, you'll find several qualified mentor prospects sitting right around you.

I want to share with you several specific characteristics that will help you identify potential mentors among the Christian women you know.

1. *Maturity.* Look for an older woman. Titus 2:3 mandates that younger women should be taught by older women. "Older" can refer to chronological age or spiritual experience. Mentors to younger moms are usually older in the Lord, having a wealth of experience with responsibility and accountability she can pass on to a younger woman. A woman in her 20s could mentor a girl in her late teens. A married woman in her late 20s could mentor a woman in her early 20s. A mother in her 30s could mentor a younger woman who has just had her first child. An older woman who has managed to raise her children alone could mentor a younger single mother who needs encouragement in the absence of a spouse. Look for someone whose maturity in the Lord is exemplary.

Let's talk for a minute about Elizabeth and Mary. In a way, Elizabeth, who was advanced in years (Luke 1:7), was a mentor to her cousin Mary, the mother of Jesus. When they were both pregnant they spent three months together (see verses 39-56).

Elizabeth had been married to Zacharias for a long time. As a young bride, Mary was able to watch how Elizabeth related to her husband. They both looked forward to bearing their children. They probably talked about babies, clothing, and everything that was required and expected of them as mothers in their culture. How Mary must have benefited from that experience!

2. *Spiritual growth.* Mentoring requires no special talent or God-given quality. But it does require someone who is willing to share her life. This woman's life, while not perfect, should reflect a desire for perfection. Yet she doesn't let her imperfections keep her from ministering to others. In her book *Out of the Saltshaker,* Becky Pippert underscores this truth: "We must not wait until we are healed first, loved first, and then reach out. We must serve no matter how well we have our act together. It may well be that one of the first steps toward our own healing will come when we reach out to someone else."[4]

3. *Wisdom.* Wisdom is a lifestyle, not a specific list of behaviors or beliefs. You can usually tell a wise woman by what she says. The Proverbs 31 woman, who is a model mentor, "opens her mouth in wisdom, and the teaching of kindness is on her tongue" (verse 26). A wise woman teaches a simple, practical way of life, a contented way of life, a life of good stewardship.

You can also tell a wise woman by what she doesn't say. She is able to keep confidences. She knows when to say what and how to put a guard over her mouth and keep watch over the doors of her lips (see Psalm 141:3). She does not participate in slander and abusive speech (Colossians 3:8).

4. *Reverence.* "Charm is deceitful and beauty is vain, but a woman who fears the LORD, she shall be praised" (Proverbs 31:30). Your potential mentor should be a reverent woman, one who longs to know God better. She must be an abiding Christian. Seeking God is her way of life. She is moderate and temperate in her behavior, a woman who monitors her own life carefully. She is not excessive in any area. Her reverent lifestyle should lead a younger mom to God and His Word.

5. *Availability.* A good mentor will not get involved in mentoring for selfish reasons. Rather, she desires to be available and to share in a younger mom's life by being transparent with her. She desires to listen with a receptive heart and to share what she knows in order

to nurture others. A true mentor will give herself wholeheartedly to serve the younger woman she is mentoring.

Elisabeth Elliot tells a wonderful story of her encounter with a mentor-type at Prairie Bible Institute (PBI). Elisabeth moved to PBI in 1948. It's a campus of very stark wooden buildings on the bleak prairie in Alberta, Canada.

"I only felt displaced and lonesome for a few weeks," Elisabeth relates. "One afternoon there came a knock on my door. I opened it to find a beautiful, rosy-cheeked face framed by white hair. The woman spoke with a charming Scottish accent. 'You don't know me, but I know you. I've been praying for you. If ever you'd like a cup of tea and a Scottish scone, just pop down to my little apartment.'"

Mrs. Cunningham became Mom Cunningham to Elisabeth. Mom Cunningham schooled her, not through classes or seminars and not primarily through words but in the classroom of the heart. She taught Elisabeth by her example that she was available to God. She had surrendered her time and was willing to get involved with others. Mom Cunningham was available to develop a burden for Elisabeth, pray for her, and then reach out to her.[5]

Look for a woman who limits the number of moms she agrees to mentor. A mentor needs to be free to give whatever it takes to help the younger mom become more confident in her relationships and skills. If she's already involved with a number of other women, she may not have enough time for you.

how does a mentoring relationship get started?

No woman is perfect. Look for someone who is earnestly seeking to fulfill the biblical model, then prayerfully and respectfully approach her. She will be a worthy guide to the path you have chosen.

Ideally, older women will initiate the mentoring relationship themselves. This is Paul's mandate to older women in Titus 2:3-5. But don't be afraid to take the initiative to invite a respected older woman to lunch or coffee just to get better acquainted. It just may be the opening she has been waiting for to approach you.

I know from talking with them that many older women are also hesitant to enter into a mentoring relationship with younger moms like yourself. The two most common reasons I find are fear and an unwillingness to give up freedom.

By the time they are 40 to 45, many women have spent the majority of their adult life raising children, serving others, and being involved in church and community life. With their own children grown (or nearly grown), they feel they have earned a little peace and quiet. They're free of major child-raising responsibilities, so they begin to find things to do to satisfy themselves. They get a little selfish and self-indulgent. Some go back to work. They don't want to give up their cherished free time to take on a younger woman.

You can ease this concern in a prospective mentor by assuring her that you don't intend to monopolize her time. For example, tell her that you're willing to get together once a week for lunch. Beyond that, you can spend more time together only if she's comfortable with it.

The second reason for hesitancy is fear. Many older women are not teachers or Bible scholars. They're afraid of being in a mentor relationship with a younger woman because they don't feel they have any knowledge to pass on or they don't feel qualified to impart knowledge to a younger mom.

These women are wrong. They need to know that you're not looking for a teacher or a Bible scholar. If you were, you could find a classroom situation for that kind of study. Encourage the older woman in your life that her experience and perspective are the best resources for sharing about life and the principles that Titus 2:3-5 suggests that younger moms learn.

As the stay-at-home movement grows, hopefully more and more churches will offer programs to get mentors and moms together. A dear sister of mine and I have been privileged to launch such a program, called "Mentors and Mothers." We created a curriculum based on the biblical principle in Titus 2:3-5 and the mentoring principles mentioned in this chapter.

In our first session we linked 14 mentors with 14 younger women. The course provided direction and teaching along with focused one-on-one time. At the end of the first 12-week session the mentors and moms wanted to stay together. How thrilled we were! The response confirmed to us the need for older women ministering in the lives of younger women. Perhaps you would like to encourage the women in your church to begin a mentoring program. If you want more suggestions for mentoring, you might refer to my book *Mentors for Mothers*.[6]

My Aunt Pat was a mentor in my life. She died more than 25 years ago. I felt so close to her that I can still go to the phone and dial her number, thinking she'll answer.

Aunt Pat provided counsel, spiritual leadership, support, challenge, and vision. She was always available. She gave me her time, her perspective, and her love. She loved God. Her recipe for lemon pound cake, her crocheted slippers, her technique for basting in a zipper, and the way she received gifts so graciously are all written on my heart. Her gifts altered the course of my life.

There's an Aunt Pat, Mom Cunningham, or Martha in your life. It may take some prayer and patient searching to discover her, but the rewards will be well worth your effort.

friendships & sisterhood

Choose carefully.

I love reading the vast array of greeting cards designed to make you see life in a comical way. Following a lesson I taught on friendship, I received a card that read:

> Without friends, the world would be a cold, lonely place, void of any real understanding or warmth—we'd be adrift, aimless and utterly alone. In other words we'd be stuck with only men to talk to.

Many books have been written about friendship, lofty idealistic volumes encouraging us to invest, share, be a friend while looking for a friend. Following a reading of this sort, I am motivated, emotional, and frankly *ready to* go out and get connected.

Relationships are God's design for being Jesus to each other. Frankly, this area of my life has caused me to stumble, and I have given others cause to be sad over my hurtful ways. Sandy Wilson, Ph.D., authored a book (now out of print) titled *Hurt People Hurt People.* Until I was able to acknowledge what I did with hurts of my past, I was hurting others along the friendship path.

Friendships with older women and younger women seemed easy

as I had a definite role. They were the teacher and I was the student or vice versa. It was my peers I struggled with. After much searching and self-knowledge, I realized I could choose my friendships, and that not everyone in the world was destined to be my best friend—or even to enter into my circle of friendships. This was the beginning of a new and healthy way to build and maintain friendships.

Once you connect with a peer, the joy and frustration of building and maintaining a friendship can be at the least difficult and at the most time-consuming and disconcerting. Who do I tell what? How soon do I tell what part of my life story? Is she trustworthy?

Choosing is only the beginning. Paul, the apostle, at the end of his life describes some friends who deserted him and some friends who showed him friendship. There are four specific measurements in his description.

The first is "refreshment." Following a visit with a friend do you feel stimulated, encouraged, loved, able to give and grow? That's refreshment.

The second is "not ashamed." I translate this phrase to ask the question, "Does this friend have an agenda for me?" Would she like me better if I did life a different way?

The third is "eagerly searched." In the culture we live in that includes the possibility of eight or more contact numbers (cell phone, land line, fax, office land line, office fax, e-mail, etc.), does this friend just "leave a message"? Oh I know, we are all glad on some occasions *just* to leave a message on the service. Is that the kind of regular relationship you want with a friend?

And fourth is "services rendered." This word, "service," changes as you grow. In early motherhood it may mean caring for your baby while you catch a nap or go the market. It may also mean the service of prayer for your family or mentoring a child of yours. The type of service changes, but service never does.

Several years ago I was privileged to be involved with a group of older women who were hosting a women's retreat in Arizona. Prior to the retreat, the group decided to spend a day together assembling retreat materials. There were seven or eight of us, and I was the youngest by at least 15 years.

As we walked around the table collecting and collating page after page of materials, the conversation of the older women drifted to their personal lives. They talked about needing eyeglasses to read the newspaper, receiving hormone injections on a regular basis, experiencing hot flashes, and living with the deepening wrinkles. I kept walking around the table with them collecting pages, but I certainly didn't feel like I was part of the conversation.

A few days later I was with a group of mothers of young children. Again the conversation focused on personal matters. They spoke of babies, deliveries, bag balm, epidurals, and elective C-sections. I was obviously the senior member of the group; I wasn't a young mom at that point. I couldn't relate to the conversation directly. At that point in my life I was a "tweener"—somewhere between babies and hot flashes. But I, too, had been on the delivery table. I had experienced labor (24 hours of it, in case anyone is interested!). I could relate to these women because I had been there.

Today, quite a few years later, I am able to relate better to the group of older sisters. My reading glasses are strewn all around the house and it seems hotter everywhere I go.

As I think about these experiences, I realize that we go through phases in our lives as moms. At every phase we find other women who are at the same place we are. We draw ourselves to women who are experiencing the same kinds of things we are experiencing, and we gain strength from our sisters.

The comic strip "It's a Mom's Life" once showed two mothers sipping coffee on the sofa with their three children being "angels." One mother, Katie, says to the other, Carol, "The kids are so much better behaved since I quit my job." The friend responds, "Yes, Katie, I think you really made the right choice." The next frame shows Katie with all the children crying and fighting, and she is phoning Carol to ask, "Could you tell me again all those good reasons I'm staying home with my children?"

We need each other to reinforce the good decisions we make. We need reminders about our principles. Any principle we sell out for an emotion is not a principle. There are times when all we need is a sister to remind us of what we already know.

At-home mom, you are not alone. You have sisters, kindred spirits for mutual support, recognition, instruction, affirmation, and fun.

friendship ingredients

Let's talk about sisterhood. What is it? Dr. Beth Brown, of Denver's Conservative Baptist Seminary, wrote her dissertation on women and friendship. She says there are six common, valued aspects of friendship among women.

First, *similarity*. Women look for other women who share their values and interests.

Second, *complementary*. Women seek to find some attributes in their friends that are different from, yet enhancing to, their own.

Third, *reciprocity and mutual support*. A woman wants to know that if she is sick her friend will bring a meal for her family, and that she can reciprocate.

Fourth, *compatibility*. A woman needs to feel at ease around her friends so she can be herself.

Fifth, *proximity*. A friend needs to be accessible. It helps if she lives close by or at least close enough to make a phone call.

Sixth, a woman looks for a *role model* in her friendships. She wants to become friends with women she respects and whose examples she can follow.

And to this list, I add a seventh: A friend *celebrates your dreams and passions*.

Weave a shared commitment to Christ into the fabric of friendship described by Dr. Brown and you have what I call sisterhood. Sister-hood is friendship plus Christ.

As an at-home mom, you need at least one sister who has chosen to stay at home as you have. The idea is not to find someone exactly like you. Rather, find another mom who shares your values about staying at home but who has some attributes that complement yours.

How do you find a sister? First, pray and ask God to give you such a woman. Ask Him to bring you a friend in a supernatural way, a woman He would drop on your doorstep. God has done that for me with four or five women at various times in my life in various cities. I remember clearly how God brought Grace to me in a small town in New Mexico. There she was, standing at my door. Later He brought Martha and Shery and still later Annie J. and Susan. God dropped them into my lap, made them available to me, and made me available to them. I took the step of initiating the relationship with each of them, but they were available.

Jan Alexander came into my life when Anissa was about two years old. Jan had two children; the oldest was three and the youngest was five months. Jan and I walked together, talked together, cried together, folded diapers together, cooked meals together, and spent time together as sisters in Christ talking about how God was using our children to refine us. Jan's friendship was an illustration to me of God's graciousness and provision. Jan was a true sister. Did we have fun!

Later, in a different city and season of my life, a group called Chaber (bound together for life) and some extraordinary women offered friendship and sisterhood. Holly, Kay, Sandy, Carol, and Sheryl invested deeply in me and allowed me to invest in their lives. The gift has been immeasurable. With aging comes years of friend-ship and the loss of friendship. I have just experienced the death of a peer for the first time, and I will never be the same.

You may be very close to your parents or your children, yet you still need a supportive sister outside your family. Many years ago I met a woman who proudly proclaimed that her mother was her best friend. Her mother was very ill and about to go home to be with Jesus. I was intrigued at that time (Anissa was 11) and thought, *How wonderful to have arrived at the age of 50 and to be able to say that your mother is your best friend in life.*

I made a lunch date with this woman to talk with her about how her mother became her best friend. We pursued this line of conversation for a couple of hours. I came to the conclusion that I didn't really want to be Anissa's best friend in life. Instead, I wanted her to have friends her own age at every stage of her life, peers who walked the same road at the same time. I had walked those steps already, and we could not walk them together. I am Anissa's mother, the older woman in her life. While I hope to be around for counsel, direction, and a strong connection, I pray that her best friends will be her peers, women who are walking the road with her.

principles for sisters

So find a sister. Ask God to send you one, then initiate and develop a relationship with her. After you have found a sister, what's next? How are you going to be in relationship with her? Here are some important guidelines.

1. *Share the same belief system.* A natural start in a sisterhood relationship is building a spiritual base. Pray that your sister will have a heart that strives for God as yours does. Pray that the two of you will be serious in matters concerning the Father and that your relationship will be based on the authority of God's Word.

We all need somebody to lean on. That's the theme of a popular song, but it has a biblical base. There are many "one another" commands in God's Word: pray for one another, love one another, exhort one another, admonish one another, be transparent with one another, confess to one another, bear one another's burdens. By following these commands your relationship with your friend will become an expression of Christ's love (see John 13:34-35).

Spiritually based friendships promote spiritual growth. In their book *Kindred Spirits,* Alice Lawhead and Kathy Narramore contend, "It seemed God planned for us to do our spiritual and emotional maturing in relationships with others."[1]

Growth takes place in the context of relationships. Abiding friendships are designed to promote our growth toward maturity by helping us see God in ourselves. They can also help meet our deep emotional needs as we accept, care for, encourage, and give to one another. When we do this for one another, we reflect the Lord to one another. Therefore we call this kind of friendship a godly friendship, a godly sisterhood.

Relational growth requires that we learn to love one another despite our imperfections. That's the true test of love.

Gilbert Tennant, an eighteenth-century preacher, colorfully described this level of love:

> In every one of our lives there's a can of worms. Believe you me! There's a skeleton in the closet of every life here. And, you see, we can be known or we can be willing to know up to that point. That's it. That's safe, but superficial...You must love right in and through that painful area, right in and through that painful point, love right on to the end. Refuse to let go, though you know everything about that person...Fragile love will love up to a point—and that's not worth anything. That's what most Christians experience. But those who are willing to know and willing to be known to the point where they go crashing right on through that threshold of pain, to where they really know and are known.[2]

2. *Be supportive.* I was recently camping with my husband in a park in California. While on a hike we came upon a huge, flat outcropping of rock about 40 feet wide. Worn into the top of the rock was a series of equal-sized indentations where Indian women ground corn for hundreds of years. It was a job each woman had to do, and it could have been done alone. But they gathered on the rock to enjoy each other's presence as they worked. It must have made the work of making cornmeal much more enjoyable. They came together as sisters,

understanding the value of support while doing a task together. Even shopping at the market is more fun with a sister.

Donna Partow, author of *No More Lone Ranger Moms,* advocates this supportive, sharing approach, using co-ops for babysitting, cleaning, even cooking. Donna writes, "I have tried motherhood both ways—as a Lone Ranger mom and as a part of a community. I now realize that many American women have made this mother- hood trip much lonelier than God intended."[3]

Single moms especially would benefit from the support and friendship provided by mentors and sisters in Christ. Seek out other moms in church groups, play groups, or at your child's school. Join or form a support group and share your experiences with other moms.

The medium of art found in paintings always resonates to a deep place in my heart. Vincent Van Gogh, for his painting called "Boats on the Beach at Saints Marie de la mer," painted on this beach for one month and watched with keen interest the fishermen, their boats, and their relationships. He titled one of the boats "Friends" and was quoted as saying about the activity among the men, "There was mutual support with singleness of purpose." Two women immersed in the same work, each doing it their way yet supporting one another—this kind of mutual support will bring about acceler- ated spiritual growth and healthy relationships.

This support will give you freedom to be transparent, authentic, and vulnerable.

3. *Be serious.* Be serious about what you are learning from one another as sisters. Be serious about your relationship as it grows. Be serious with one another about things that matter.

Not long ago I realized that a dear friend and I, who have been through thick and thin together, had a tension point. We had devel- oped a strong, open relationship, and we were blunt and direct with each other at times. But something was wrong.

Because we love each other, we sat down one day to talk it out. We discovered that part of the problem was this forthrightness we've always expressed. We decided that we had stepped over the line of respect for one another through our bluntness. Of all the people in the world to hurt! We cherished each other deeply, and we wanted to make certain that our cherishing was evident in everything we said. But we had been speaking the truth without proper doses of love.

The right to be frank and forthright with each other is a great gift. But it is not a frivolous thing; it is not to be taken lightly. It is to be given and taken seriously.

Sisterhood brings comfort, encouragement, and shared experiences. But sisterhood takes time and energy, and that's a serious matter.

4. *Be silly.* Being serious about your relationship doesn't mean you shouldn't have fun. On the contrary, as sisters you should be lighthearted, joyful, and sometimes even silly with one another.

I have a dear friend named Joan, and we occasionally go to a movie together. We like the soft and corny ones, you know, the "PG" love stories that our husbands are rarely interested in. And we always go to the cheap showings.

Recently Joan and I headed for a before-six o'clock movie. She dropped me off at the door so I could find two seats in the theater while she parked the car. It was pitch dark inside the theater, of course, so it took a few minutes for my eyes to adjust to the dark. I spotted two seats in the crowded theater and charged ahead. I climbed over two or three people and sat down. "My friend is coming," I said, warning them that Joan would soon be tripping over them to find her seat.

After my eyes became accustomed to the darkness, I turned to see Joan enter the theater. I could see her by the light of the screen, but she was blind to me. I began to wave a scrap of paper at her hoping to attract her attention. She couldn't see it. The lady behind me began waving her handkerchief at Joan. No luck. Soon there were three hankies in the air, then the whole row got involved.

Finally, in desperation I whispered loudly, "Joan, I'm over here!" Her voice came back, "I can hear you, but I can't see you."

At that point everyone in the surrounding area, no doubt fed up with the sideshow, pitched in and helped Joan find the right seat. Of course, she tripped over the people sitting next to us. We giggled as silently as we could. Amazingly, not one person around us found any fault; they were all very gracious. I think we were more entertaining than the movie.

Don't make everything in your relationship serious. Be silly with your friend. Giggle a bit, laugh a lot. Look for things to make you laugh together. Lightheartedness is the perfect balance to the serious side of your friendship.

I once saw a T-shirt with the caption: "I have faith that one day I will reach my goal and weigh what my driver's license says I do." That's my idea of humor. My sisters think it's funny too.

Various organizations, such as my Homemakers By Choice, provide connecting places for moms.

In *To Understand Each Other*, Dr. Paul Tournier, an M.D. and Swiss psychiatrist, wrote wonderful insights on communication:

> How beautiful, how grand and liberating this experience is, when people learn to help each other. It is impossible to overemphasize the immense need humans have to be really listened to, to be taken seriously, to be understood.
>
> Modern psychology has brought it very much to our attention. At the very heart of all psychotherapy is this type of relationship in which one can tell everything, just as a little child will tell all to his mother.
>
> No one can develop freely in this world and find a full life without feeling understood by at least one person....
>
> He who would see himself clearly must open up to a confidant freely chosen and worthy of such trust.
>
> Listen to all the conversations of our world, between nations as well as t hose between couples. They are for the most part dialogues of the deaf.[4]

Friendships matter. Choose carefully.

a final word: the best return on your investment

What will be the outcome of all you do as an at-home mom? You may be so busy with the day-to-day whirlwind that it's hard for you to see any of the results of staying at home. But others have been down the road ahead of you, and they have reaped the dividends of the years they invested as stay-at-home moms. I hope the words of one of these moms will be an encouragement to you:

"Investment" is a term with which most of us are familiar. We frequently hear about short-term investments, long-term investments, money markets, IRAs, stocks, bonds, etc.

I have been investing most of my life—not that I have exchanged money for a gamble in the stock market. No, I have been investing in people, three people who are very important to me. I speak of my three daughters, and I consider the time and effort I have invested in them to be the most significant work I have ever done.

I haven't always felt this way. There were days when I gladly would have traded places with a ditch digger. Those were the days when the kids had the chicken pox, the dishwasher ran over, and the teacher called to discuss my child's grades. They were the days when the siblings demonstrated the depth of their rivalry, neglected their chores, and sassed me when I reminded them. There wasn't much return on my investment of time and effort those days. At such times, I wondered whether I'd make it through 20 years, much less have anything to show for it if I did.

It is only as we take stock of our assets that we are reassured. We have the hugs and kisses, the excited invitations to "come and see," the homemade cards and gifts, the days when our kids say, "You're the best mom in the whole world!"

That isn't all. For me, the returns really began to be realized when my children were grown. When they internalized my values, I felt that my investment of time in training and modeling was returned with interest. When they began to share my values with others, I was rewarded amply. When they grew into mature yet always growing individuals, I could not have been prouder. When they taught me things I didn't know or hadn't considered, my investment was paid in full.

Much media attention has been focused on the growing hesitance of American couples to have children. Such reports trouble me. These people do not see raising children as a worthwhile investment. They see the costs, but not the returns. They understand the sacrifices, but do not comprehend the joy of giving, the privilege of training and loving another human being.

It takes vision, even faith, to see the returns ahead of time. It takes commitment to give ourselves to such a long-term involvement. We have to see it as an investment, not only for ourselves, but also for the world. Seeing the results of our efforts can be the most fulfilling experience of our entire lives.[1]

When I begin some of my conference sessions with moms, I announce, "You will not learn anything today." The audience moans audibly. I quickly add, "You only learn something by doing it. When you do it, it belongs to you." Similarly, you won't learn anything from this book until you put it into practice. So practice, practice, practice, and you will begin to see your investment as an at-home mom grow.

The common begin, the uncommon finish. Go out and finish strong!

A note from an at-home mom

Loving life as an at-home mom...that is my desire. But it has not been an easy journey. I, like many others in my generation, graduated from college and pursued a great career. I enjoyed the financial rewards as well as the emotional confirmations that I was doing a good job. I felt secure in knowing I could "take care of myself," as my generation of women has been strongly encouraged to do. However, after the birth of my second daughter, I felt God tugging at my heart daily that I needed to be home with my children. I believed that my husband and children would benefit more by my staying home than from my regular paycheck, which was about 50 percent of our income at the time of my decision.

After my initial decision to come home, I was overwhelmed. I wanted perfection in all areas of my life, yet I was struggling in my roles as wife, woman, mother, and most of all, homemaker. I now had to find a new identity at home and be content in this new season of my life. After leaving the workplace, I realized that some days it would have been easier to go to work than to be home all day with my children. During my work years I actually had time to think, complete projects, and go to the bathroom by myself. I have told many people that being home with my children has been the hardest job I have ever had, but it's definitely the most rewarding. I feel so blessed that God has provided for our family so that I have the opportunity to enjoy the many rewards of being home.

It has been nearly two-and-a-half years that I have been home now. Through the many blessings of a local organization (Homemakers By Choice), I have developed vital relationships with other mothers that encourage me to be proud of the choice I have made to stay at home. Most of all, the many valuable lessons I have learned about the different roles I play are helping me to continually improve the way I do things for my family. I have areas that still need some polishing, but I have witnessed God's many blessings on my choice to be a stay-at-home mom.

Michele Pace, CPA
Phoenix, AZ

notes

chapter 2—you are not alone

1. Louise Story, "Many Women at Elite Colleges Set Career Path to Motherhood," *New York Times,* September 20, 2005.
2. Deborah Fallows, *A Mother's Work* (New York: Houghton Miffin, 1985).
3. Barbara Bush, "Choices and Change," speech delivered at Severance Green, Wellesley College, Wellesley, MA, June 1, 1990.
4. "Staying at Home," *Arizona Republic,* May 12, 1991.

chapter 3—you are the best choice

1. I recommend that you read the informative article by Sandra Tsing Loh, "Rhymes with Rich: One Woman's Conscientious Objection to the 'Mommy Wars,'" in *Atlantic Monthly,* May 2006.
2. Jay Belsky, "Infant Daycare: A Cause for Concern," Family Research Council, p. 5.
3. Armand M. Nicholi, Jr., M.D., "What Do We Know About Successful Families?" excerpts from papers delivered in the 1990s.
4. Ibid.
5. Ibid.
6. Belsky, "Infant Daycare," n.p.
7. Cited in Lynn Smith and Bob Sipchen, "Parents Report Work Taking Toll on Family Life," *Los Angeles Times,* as reported in *The Register-Guard,* Eugene, OR, August 12, 1990, p. 4C.
8. Cynthia Whitfield, "Mothers Need to Know It's O.K. to Stay Home," *The Register-Guard,* Eugene, OR, May 6, 1990, p. 2C.
9. Megan Rosenfeld, "Child Rearing," *The Washington Post,* November 1986.
10. Bryna Siegel, *The Working Parent's Guide to Daycare.*

chapter 4—motherhood is a ministry!

1. A handout from Barbara Johnson, Spatula Ministries.

chapter 5—saying the "big yes" to being an at-home mom

1. http://swz.salary.com/momsalarywizard/htmls/mswl_momcenter.html, June 23, 2006.

chapter 6—cultivating character in your children

1. Transcribed from the "Focus on the Family" radio broadcast, February 14, 1991.

chapter 7—your children, loud and lovable

1. Prudence McIntosh, "The Myth of Quality Time," *Focus on the Family*, May 1986, p. 11.
2. Dean Merrill, "Pizza for Breakfast," *Focus on the Family*, July 1991, p. 2.
3. Donna Otto, *All in Good Time* (Nashville: Thomas Nelson, 1985), adapted from pp. 180-81.

chapter 8—launching your children into the future

1. Darien Cooper, *Beholding God* (Wheaton, IL: Victor Books, 1987), p. 33.

chapter 9—checking your id

1. Jeanette Clift George, *Travel Tips from a Reluctant Traveler* (Nashville: Thomas Nelson, 1987), adapted from pp. 47-51.

chapter 10—creating a dot.calm world

1. *Arizona Republic*, May 29, 2006.

chapter 11—finding time for growth

1. Marshall H. Hart, "What Do Women Do All Day?" in *Home Life Magazine*, August 1976, Sunday School Board of the Southern Baptist Convention. All rights reserved. Used by permission of the author.
2. Eileen Pollinger, "Deep Diving Ducks," source unknown.
3. Jan Johnson, "Survival Strategies for Stay-at-Home Moms," *Christian Parenting Today*, Jan./Feb. 1990, p. 32.
4. Ibid., adapted from pp. 32-35.

chapter 12—your personal places

1. Donna Otto, *All in Good Time* (Nashville: Thomas Nelson, 1985), adapted from pp. 184-86.
2. Anne Ortlund, *Disciplines of the Beautiful Woman* (Waco, TX: Word, Inc., 1977), p. 45.

chapter 14—your man is not your enemy

1. Genesis 2:24.
2. Genesis 1:28.
3. Ephesians 5:25;5:33.
4. Ephesians 5:33.
5. Matthew 19:6.

chapter 15—your home, your nest

1. Donna Otto, *All in Good Time* (Nashville: Thomas Nelson, 1985), adapted from pp. 163-64.
2. Ibid., adapted from pp. 164-66.

chapter 16—making money at home

1. "Giving Parents More Homework," *Family Policy*, Nov./Dec. 1988, adapted from pp. 1-3.

chapter 18—mentors for mothers

1. Daniel Levenson, "The Learning Dialogue: Mentoring," in J. Fried, ed., *New Directions for Student Services Education for Student Development*, no. 15 (San Francisco: Jossey-Bass, September 1981).
2. Ted Engstrom, *The Fine Art of Mentoring* (Brentwood, TN: Wolgemuth and Hyatt Publishers, Inc., 1989), p. 24.
3. Ibid., p. 28.
4. Rebecca M. Pippert, *Out of the Saltshaker* (Downers Grove, IL: InterVarsity Press, 1979).
5. The *Elisabeth Elliot Newsletter*, Sep./Oct. 1989.
6. For more information on the "Mentors and Moms" program, contact Donna Otto (see back of this book).

chapter 19—friendships & sisterhood

1. Alice Lawhead and Kathy Narramore, *Kindred Spirits* (Grand Rapids, MI: Zondervan, 1960), p. 67.
2. From a sermon by Gilbert Tennant, "Brotherly Love Recommended by the Argument of the Love of God," 1750.
3. Donna Partow, "Moms Helping Moms," *Focus on the Family* magazine, February 1996.
4. Paul Tournier. *To Understand Each Other* (Richmond, VA: John Knox Press, 1962), p. 29.

a final word

1. Barbara A. Smith, "The Twenty-Year Investment," *Welcome Home Magazine*, vol. 3, no. 12, Dec. 1986, p. 15.

Resources

Recommended Websites
Customerperspectives.com
Focus on the Family
Half.com
Hearts at Home.com
Homemakersbychoice.org
Overstock.com
Proverbs31.com

Great Books
7 Myths of Working Mothers, Suzanne Venker
101 Ways to Make Money, Gwen Ellis
As for Me and My House, Walter Wangerin, Jr.
A Grace Disguised, Gerald L. Sittser
Habits of a Child's Heart, Valerie E. Hess and Marti Watson Garlett
Hide or Seek, James Dobson
Hints on Child Training, H. Clay Trumbull
How to Really Love Your Child, Ross Campbell
Hurt People Hurt People, Sandra Wilson
Is There Really Sex After Kids? Jill Savage
Keep a Quiet Heart, Elisabeth Elliot
Making Sunday Special, Karen Mains
Mommy Where Are You? Kathi Mills
Praying for Your Children, Stormie Omartian
Rachel Ray Cook Books
Raising Kids for True Greatness, Tim Kimmel
Released from Shame, Sandra Wilson
Sacred Parenting, Gary L. Thomas
Shame-Free Parenting, Sandra Wilson
Shepherding a Child's Heart, Tedd Tripp
The Shaping of a Christian Family, Elisabeth Elliot
The Smart Mom's Guide to Staying Home, Christine Walker
What Is a Family? Edith Schaeffer

For more information on Donna Otto's ministry or if you would like to have her speak to your group, contact:

Donna Otto
11453 N. 53rd Place
Scottsdale, AZ 85254
480-991-7464

or consult her organization
Homemakers By Choice at
www.homemakersbychoice.org

HARVEST HOUSE
PUBLISHERS

99990

More Great Books
by Donna Otto

FINDING A MENTOR, BEING A MENTOR
You'll discover how to develop and nourish a healthy, supportive, fulfilling mentoring relationship. As you share the joys and pains of everyday life with another woman, you'll discover worthwhile strategies for navigating the demands of being a wife, mother, friend, and businesswoman.

FINDING YOUR PURPOSE AS A MOM
Donna shares with readers insights to help them have the home of their dreams, where holiness reigns and peace and joy can be found. You'll discover ideas to create a relaxing, loving environment, nourish bodies and souls, enjoy life with creativity and laughter, and provide a safe, peaceful place for family and guests.

SECRETS OF GETTING MORE DONE IN LESS TIME
Break free from the all-work-and-no-play lifestyle with this practical, creative, timesaving system to help you deal with clutter, deadlines, interruptions, budgets, and more. A passport to happier, healthier, and more relaxed living.

MENTORS FOR MOTHERS CURRICULUM
This special program will help you set up a mentor group or enhance your current mentoring organization.

Overton Memorial Library
Loving life as an at-home mom /
306.8743 O911 2006

99990